God Sexology:
It's Love, Marriage, Then Sex, In That Order

The Sexually Immoral Person Will Be Punished

Lamont Wall

Table of Contents

Dedication

This book is dedicated to all who can bear witness to living a sexually immoral lifestyle, who are grateful to now, be dead to such a practice by the power of God, and all who desire to know the truth that sets a person free from the bondage of sin.

Acknowledgement

I want to be sure to acknowledge the only one who made it possible for my ability to be filled with wisdom, knowledge, and understanding of the subject matter spoken of in this book, my Lord and Savior, Jesus Christ.

Introduction

Right out the gate, let me profess that I love sex! I am one of the many in society and the world that have a frequent desire for it. From my youth, watching cable television, sex became my curiosity. The naked body of a woman, seeing scenes of two people having sex in movies, planted and watered the seed of sexual immorality in my heart and increased in me a desire to experience sex. I can recall times when I would sit up at night watching the cable station, Cinemax. There was a show entitled, "Friday Night After Dark," which aired beginning at 12am. All the movies after 12am featured adult entertainment and were not suitable for anyone that was not of adult age. However, my mother was not aware of what was available for viewing on Friday nights after midnight. Therefore, I would sit up while she was asleep and watch what my young eyes or any young eyes shouldn't entertain themselves with. I saw lots of nudity, the nipples of women's breasts, vaginal pubic hair, buttocks, and many sex scenes minus visual penetration. I was so desperate to fill my eyes with sexual lusts that even when the cable got cut off due to the bill not being paid, I would still watch what I could through the lines on the TV. Yeah, you could still see somewhat although it wasn't as clear as what those who paid their cable bill could see. Eventually my curiosity would lead to a desire for more than just seeing what I was able to see watching cable TV. I wanted to see two people going all the way, the man's penis being thrusted into the woman's vagina, oral sex scenes, etc. So, when I was old enough to rent videos, I took advantage of such a privilege. I would get off work at 7am, sit around for about an hour and a half until the video store opened at 8:30am. My mom would also be at work because she worked on a 1st shift job. I was so addicted to porn that I didn't even consider watching X rated movies. Instead, I chose to watch XXX rated movies only, renting them three at a time, and watching all 3 back-to-back. When I finished watching them, I would take them back, so that no one had a clue that I'd been watching pornography. Being aroused by what I saw in the movies, at some point, during or after watching them I would sexually satisfy myself.

Indeed, pornography and masturbation were my addictions for many years of my teenage to young adult life. Without a doubt, evil was my influence at an early age, during a time when I was ignorant to the truth about God and His standard for sexuality. However, my experience is also the experience of many others in the world. Things associated with sexual immorality are all around us and out of curiosity and for the pleasure thereof, people are entertaining themselves with such things. As a result, many are enslaving themselves. Fortunately, I now know what I didn't know then, and therefore, I can appreciate the mercy God showed me in my ignorance. No, my life wasn't changed by my own might or power, but it was the truth that I heard from above that set me free. I am writing this book to expose sexual immorality and reveal God's standard for sex which comes with no consequences. First, I will establish that there is a God, and we are His offspring, and He alone establishes our purpose unto His glory, honor, and praise. Hopefully, after reading this book, you will desire the freedom from the bondage of sexual immorality that I now have in God, my Savior.

CHAPTER 1
The Foundation of the Truth

I've been in the world for 51 years now and what I've come to realize is that there is the truth and there is the lie. There is also that which is good and that which is evil. Furthermore, there is the righteous thing to do and there is the unrighteous thing to do. When it comes to some things, you just can't have one without the other; one reveals what the other is not. Because of this, if you know what is good to do, you will also have the knowledge of what is not good to do. If you know what is right to do, you will also have the knowledge of what is not right to do. The same principle applies to distinguishing between what is true and what is not. Since such things are established by one greater than who is required to receive the truth, that the founder of all truth, can also be the one who directs the path of those who hear what His will is. Only the will of God is non-discriminatory and applies to all people the same. Indeed, we the people, would like to have the authority to define for ourselves the reality we desire. The problem with this is, if the decision is left up to us to set standard for living, we would never agree on what is best for us all, which is why the world is filled with people simply doing their own thing. Except we agree, we can't walk together. Perhaps that explains the division and chaos in the world. Because of sin, there is the existence of selfishness, which all people are guilty of. We all have our own desires and what we desire, we have the tendency to encourage others to desire also. For this reason, mankind doesn't qualify as the foundation of truth. Besides, none of us can take credit for our own existence or the existence of others.

He is God who made us all and no one is equal to Him. So, let us revere Him who knew us before we were in our mother's womb. The word of God tells us in the book of John and in the book of Revelation concerning his existence. It is revealed to us that God alone has no beginning of days nor ending of days, no father or mother (Revelation 1:8, 11). The evidence is clearly written in the book of John, Chapter 1, and verse 1-3 that in the beginning God and His Word exist and He is responsible for all that exists. In other words, He alone has no creator, because He was before anything was or could be. According to what is written, He created heaven and the earth and everything in them both (Genesis 1:1; Colossians 1:16). Furthermore, if it exists, it was also created for Him. Everything seen and unseen belongs to Him. The power of God is unmatchable! He is the only Being that can speak things that do not exist into existence just as Romans, Chapter 4 and 17 indicates. We also witness Him doing just that in Genesis, chapter 1, verses 3-14. His word has the power to give life and to keep alive, and to kill, and what He speaks never returns unto Him void, but if He speaks a thing it will come to pass. This too, is revealed to us in the word of God (2 King 5:7; Isaiah 55:11; Acts 5:3-5, 7-10; Luke 11:43-44).

It is foolish for a person to choose to walk in disobedience to an Almighty God, whose existence is clearly seen by what He has made. God doesn't change His mind. He will do what He says He will do. Unlike people, God cannot lie according to Numbers 23:19. Neither can He do evil or tempt anyone to do it. Therefore, no one can blame God for the evil they do, which means that we are all individually held accountable for our actions. It is also important that we know that every path, every place that man plants his feet on earth, God sees. He is an all-wise God, also. For this reason, it is important for us to acknowledge the power of God. Ask any person who is alive in the world if they can remember the day they were in their mother's womb like God can! Not even our parents know the exact moment when it happened, but God does. As far as the day we entered the world, only those who witnessed it can tell us the exact day and time when we were born. However, we ourselves have no memory of certain things pertaining to our own life. We have no right to question the will of an all-seeing and all-knowing God. What He says from His mouth is true and unapologetic. Absolutely nothing He says can be overturned or changed by anyone. Not only does His word change not, and it never returns unto Him ineffective. Instead, if He speaks, what proceeds from His mouth shall come to pass. Those who believe in God and accept Him as the Lord of their life will perceive His word to be true and come to realize that the word of every man is not to be trusted. The wise will lean not on their own understanding, as the book of proverbs 3:5-6 states. The desire of our heart will be to trust in the Lord who alone directs our path. Our obedience to Him will lead to our purpose being fulfilled and Him being glorified.

As the Creator, God understands existence better than anyone. Therefore, He alone knows what is best for us. God doesn't have to study existence to come up with a hypothesis. He is the author of all that is. We need only to be willing to hear from Him the things that pertain to our life and our body. We do not need years of research when we can seek God, who is a rewarder of them who diligently seek Him, according to Hebrews 11:6. Neither is He hard to find, because According to Acts 17:27, we can seek Him and He is not far from anyone. We have no excuse. If we seek Him, we shall find Him because He is not far from anyone. Our obedience to Him rewards us with knowledge, wisdom, and understanding, which things that the fool doesn't care to know because it proves their way to be not according to the truth that comes from God. This is revealed to us in proverbs, Chapter 1, and verse 7 and 22. Severe consequence is the outcome of people doing their own will rather than the will of God, as Solomon also writes (Proverbs 14:12). The fact that we only exist because of the Creator, the least that we could do is live unto His glory, honor, and praise. Let us glorify Him by hearing and obeying Him as Lord of our life. Then and only then is our Lord pleased with what He has made.

Although it is not His will that any of His offspring should perish, such will be the outcome of the soul that is clear on what the will of the Lord is but refuses to turn unto God in repentance. Our

Father is a God of love, which is why Peter emphasizes the importance of repentance, which the Lord Himself says, is the only thing that can keep a person from perishing (2 Peter 3:9; Luke 13:1-5). In the sight of God, the disobedient is unworthy of Him. He or she proves by their actions that they do not love God with their whole heart, soul, and mind, which is what the word of God says is the greatest command (Matthew 22:37). Jesus also said, and I paraphrase, "any person who doesn't love Him more than anyone else, is not worthy of Him" (Matthew 10:37). Hopefully, you can see that if the thing that is made doesn't, please the one who made it, it is worthless. Therefore, if we fail to live out our purpose for existing, what good is our existence! Can you see from this that we were not simply made. Because we did not make ourselves, we ought not think that we can do what we choose to do without reaping consequences for our rebellious behavior. Besides, can we say that a parent who doesn't discipline their children, loves them? Absolutely not! The word of God teaches discipline as an act of love and/or the lack thereof as the absence of love (Proverbs 13:24; Hebrews 12:6).

God loves us and wants to fellowship with us and wants to be pleased with us! So, let us acknowledge Him as the foundation of truth. Let us humble ourselves before Him, and He shall direct our path. Indeed, we are all knowingly guilty of something God is not pleased with at some point in life. This too, is revealed to us in the word of God. According to Romans 3:23-24, "we have all sinned and come short of the glory of God" and we can all receive grace and forgiveness unto eternal life (Romans 3:23-24). Life is a gift to us, and God did not consult with us to see if we had a desire to exist before deciding to create us. His action proves that He has no one to answer to. Besides, if living wasn't a good thing or something all who are alive doesn't want to continue doing, none of us would have ever been born into the world. However, if we are honest with ourselves, we all agree that life is a good thing, even if some refuse to live in obedience to God.

I can't say that I know a single person who truly doesn't want to exist anymore for the right reason. Indeed, we know of instances where people have committed suicide, but no one has ever said, "I am going to kill myself because I didn't ask to be born." The only thing that truly drives a person to end a good thing is the inability to have the kind of life that they desire in their heart, void of the consequences that follow a disobedient life. Ultimately, no one truly wants to die and because of sin, death will come for us at its appointed time. God is not going to tolerate a sinful world forever. All flesh will die, saith the Lord in the first book of the bible, Genesis 3:19 and Hebrews 9:27. According to what is written, even the world as a whole and all the pleasures of the world, will pass away and come to an end at the pass of each day (1 John 2:17). God also gives us a glimpse of what will eventually happen to those who refuse to repent of what he hates. It is in Genesis, Chapter 6 and verse 17 that we read, "And behold, I, even I, do bring a flood of waters upon the earth, to destroy all flesh, wherein is the breath of life, from under the heaven; and everything that is in the earth shall die." This is not something done without a valid reason. Remember, He has no intention of destroying anyone. However, when people are commanded to turn from a lifestyle that God hates and they refuse, God has no choice but to destroy them. In fact, He gives us the reason why the destruction was necessary in verses 5, 12, and 13. God was displeased with all the wickedness in the heart of the unrepentant, and the corruption and violence in the earth.

As you can also see, even death serves a purpose. God desires to have a kingdom where all the citizens thereof walk in absolute obedience to Him. The world as it is not the kingdom of God because of sin, and therefore, it will eventually be destroyed, but no one is destined to be in a state of total separation from God. Each person will decide to follow Christ or not to, and it will be their own decision that condemns them. What is obvious is, people die every day. What is also obvious is, there is an end to these bodies of flesh which is forever at conflict with the will of God. The fact that we die also means that there is an eternal place for the souls of men. However, there is one for the righteous, those who obey God and another for the unrighteous, those who refuse to obey Him. This is revealed to us in the book of John, Chapter 3, and verse 16. The verse teaches us the reward of believing in Jesus and the consequence for refusing to. According to the verse, those who believe shall not perish. Instead, they shall have everlasting life. On the other hand, those who refuse to believe shall perish.

The word perish indicates that there will be punishment for the unrighteous. According to Revelation 21:8, there will be a second death suffered by those whose names are not written in the Lamb's book of life. For this reason, Jesus didn't waste any time telling the people to repent in Matthew, Chapter 4, and verse 17. Truthfully, a person who has a desire to know the truth, will not see a call to repentance as a message of hate or one that is intended to condemn people. Instead, they will understand it to be a message of love. Jesus made it clear that He did not come into the world to condemn the word, but that through Him the world might be saved (John 3:17). God is not simply telling us that we are doomed to hell. Rather He is telling us, "If we refuse to repent, then we shall perish." So, we are not forced to perish, we choose to perish by choosing what pleases the flesh rather than God. Therefore, it is imperative that we desire the gift of God, which is eternal life.

In the new world that God Himself shall establish, death shall exist no more and the people in it will not have to exercise freewill, but shall continue doing the will of God free from temptation. Unfortunately, the disobedient will have nothing to look forward to after this life is over. The life they try to keep, Jesus said, they shall lose (Matthew 16:25-26). Paul, in his letter to Timothy made it clear that we entered the world without possession, and we will leave the world in a like manner. God cannot lie! Whatever He speaks will come to pass. The consequence for refusing to obey God is written in multiple places throughout the word of God for a reason. I encourage you to read 1 Corinthians 6:9-10; Galatians 5:19-21; and Revelation 21:8, just to name a few. Now is the only opportunity that we must hear the truth and obey.

The kingdom of God is the greatest blessing that anyone can receive. We're talking about a new body and a better life that shall be void of anything that people can suffer in this life. Be willing to give it all up in exchange for the gift of eternal life in the life to come and treasure riches that can't rot or decay or be stolen away (Matthew 6:19-20; Luke 9:23)! One thing is for sure, the only thing better than having the opportunity to live temporarily in these earthly bodies, is someday being granted the opportunity to live forever in a new celestial body, that is spoken of in 1 Corinthians 15:52-57). I am certainly looking forward to the freedom from all the suffering of pain and sorrow that is experienced in this life. All we must do is, hear and obey the word of God. Is that too much for God to ask! Surely, no one deserves a reward for bad behavior.

Not even a good parent would be willing to reward their children's disobedience. If we could do whatever we choose to do and still receive the gift of eternal life, God Himself would be meaningless and the fool could rightfully say, "there is no God." Thankfully, the existence of God is clear to us all. Although some might pretend that they are not aware of the truth and succeed at fooling people, the Almighty God no one can fool. So, let us revere Him who knew us before we were in our mother's womb. From this point on, I will deal with God's biblical standard for sexuality. In the next chapter you will learn the purpose for the existence of the male and female gender.

CHAPTER 2
The Purpose of Male and Female

Mankind didn't just appear out of thin air. By now, you cannot deny that we are all the creation of God. Although it is true that God speaks things into existence, not all of us were born into the world unto a biological father and mother as newborns. Initially, God forms an adult male which is written in Genesis 1:7. Then, we read of God making a companion for the man in Chapter 2. In verse 18 we can see that it was God's idea to create man a companion. The proceeding verses reveal the creation of a woman for the man whom God brought to the man, to see what the man would call her. It is important that we don't overlook the fact that God created a female companionship for the man. The relationship was not simply a friendship kind of relationship but a joining of two people of the opposite sex together as one, which is indicated in verses 23-24. Also, the kind of relationship that Adam shared with Eve, is for people of adult age only, who can live without parental supervision, which is emphasized in verse 24. Such a relationship consists of one male adult and one female adult, and children do not qualify as suitable companions, which we shall discuss much later. The purpose of a male and female is necessary for the sake of procreation. If we look at Genesis 1:28, we can see that God's purpose for making a man and a woman was bigger than solving the problem of loneliness. It is the will of God that the earth be filled with people. For this purpose, it is written in verse 27, "So God created man in his own image, in the image of God created he him; male and female created he them." So, we have the creation of male and female. Then, we have the reason both are necessary revealed to us in verse 28. There, we find the words, "And God blessed them, and God said unto them, be fruitful, and multiply, and replenish the earth." God has a will that can only be accomplished by a male and a female sexual relationship, which is what the words, "Be fruitful and multiply," is implying that they should do. We first read of a man knowing a woman in Genesis, chapter 4. When it says, "Adam knew Eve, it is implying that he engaged in sexual intercourse with her (1). As a result of engaging in sex, the woman became pregnant and eventually gave birth, who became pregnant and gave birth. The male and the female although both are a part of mankind, they have differences that are also necessary to point out. Indeed, they are both a part of mankind. They are the same in that regard. However, the fact that it takes one male and one female to accomplish procreation, there must be something that males have that females don't. It's just like plugging a cord into an outlet and once the two are joined as one, energy is then generated. All men are born with what identifies a man as a male. Scientifically, it's called a penis. Likewise, all women have certain identifiers associated with females. They are all born with what is scientifically called a vagina.. The male's penis and the female's vagina accomplishes reproduction when they are joined together during sexual intercourse. In a sense, the man is the cord that plugs into the woman who is the outlet. It is the man that releases sperm from himself into the woman where fertilization takes place and pregnancy happens. Once she is pregnant, the child immediately grows and develops inside of her. The life inside of her is eventually delivered into the world where it becomes a part of the human race. Another way to look at it is, the man is the farmer who plants his seed, and the woman is the fertile soil where the seed is planted and grows until maturity.

There is absolutely no other way that God created for a person to be born into the world than by sexual intercourse. The truth doesn't change because someone refuses to accept it. People will continue to be naturally born into the world one way. Our God is a God of order. He doesn't agree with any relationship that deviates from His natural order. Not even Jesus as Lord came into the world different from us. According to what is written in the book of Isaiah, Chapter 7 and verse 14, Jesus came into the world through the womb of a woman. What is spoken in the book of Isaiah is also confirmed and fulfilled in the first chapter of the book of Matthew, verse 18. If it is God's will that a man and a woman have children, we can also conclude that it is also God's will that a man only has natural affection for a woman. God created one mate for Adam, which is also of the same kind, but of the opposite sex. For the sake of clarity, we will discuss forbidden sexuality and the restriction God put in place.

CHAPTER 3
Their Sexual Boundary that We Must Not Cross

The reproduction process is restricted to the same kind. God has placed boundaries that should not be crossed by anyone. God could have given Adam an animal companion or another male companion, but He specifically created a woman to be his companion. In fact, the woman was the only companion suitable for the man because the man could accomplish with her what he could not accomplish with another man or any other creature. God was able to fill the earth with more people by Adam engaging in sexual intercourse with his wife Eve. This being so, a human's sexual involvement with another created kind ought not be. A man's sexual involvement with anyone or anything other than a woman goes against the natural order, and if unnatural it also goes against the will of God. God made sure that no one is confused about forbidden sexuality. According to Leviticus 20:15-16; Deuteronomy 27:21, we are told clearly not to have sex with animals (beast). If God disapproves of the relationships, those who ignore the restriction are guilty of sexual sin. They are sexually immoral until they die to the desires of their flesh and humbly walk in obedience to God. The chance of a person having sex with an animal and not knowing it is wrong is not possible. There are just some things that we do not have to be taught. Furthermore, God has created us with a conscience that we might feel conviction when we do things that we should do. We are given a written example of this in the book of Romans. Paul says this about the Gentiles. He said, "For when the Gentiles, which have not the law, do by nature the things contained in the law, these having not the law, are a law unto themselves: Which shew the work of the law written in their hearts, their conscience also bearing witness, and their thoughts the mean while accursing or else excusing one another" (2:14-15). It must also be understood that God judges the hidden secrets of the heart, including the thoughts and intents (v. 16; Hebrews 4:12) Although bestiality is obviously sin, a desire for sexual pleasure has driven many across the established boundary. Further prove that people are aware that sex with animals is wrong; they do it secretly because they don't want anyone to know that they do such a thing. The truth is, most would be embarrassed or ashamed if they were caught in the act or if anyone knew about their secret. Now, be honest! Would you be OK with those closest to you knowing that you enjoy sexual pleasure with animals! Of course not! Will it not also bother you to witness a person having sex with an animal! Of course, it would if you have any morals! Very few people would dare to tell you that they enjoy it and are not ashamed.

There is also another sexual sin like unto it, bestiality that ought not be done by us. God has also set a boundary that is within the human race. Human sexuality is indeed a good thing, but only when it is done according to the natural order. We've already established that God gave man a woman companion to enjoy sex with and for the sake of birthing more people in the world. Unfortunately, there are those who disobey the obvious natural order and have vile affection toward people of the same sex. Well, the word of God reveals the will of God and exposes the things that God hates. When it comes to who we can engage in sin with, there can be no confusion. If God is against it, we should be able to find the truth concerning it written in some place in the word of God. Now, the question is, is it clearly stated any place in the word of God that God is against same sex relations? Proving everything by the word of God is important, because in doing so, we refute all people's opinions that contradict what God said. God's view on same sex relationships is also found in various places through the word of God. Before I provide what is written in the book of Leviticus and Deuteronomy and a few other places. I want to make mention of an incident that occurred in the days of Lot. Genesis 19:4 speaks of the young and old men of the city Lot was living in, coming to his house.

The same men made it clear to Lot what they wanted in verse 5. According to the verse, the men of the city wanted Lot to bring the men (who were angels) out of his house so that they might know them. Now, the words, "know them" are not referring to becoming familiar with them or wanting to know who they are or where they were from. Remember, "know them" carries the same meaning as Genesis 4:1 where it tells us that Adam knew his wife. The men of the city were implying that they wanted to have sex with the men in Lot's house. verse 7 confirms that their interest was sex. Perhaps some would argue that the passage is not speaking about same sex, but if you drop down to verse 8, we are told that Lot offered the men of the city his two virgin daughters for sexual pleasure, but the men had no desire for women. Just by this alone, we know that God is not in support of same sex relationships. Also, Lot referred to the sexual desire of the men as a wicked thing (v. 7).

God's disapproval is clearly stated in other places also. Leviticus 20:13 says it this way, "If a man also lies with mankind, as he lieth with a woman, both of them have committed an abomination: they shall surely be put to death; their blood shall be upon them." Surely this is clear, and if God is against a man having sexual intercourse with another man, he is also against a woman having sex with another woman. Although this is not mentioned in the book of Leviticus, we know by what is written that God is not a respecter of persons. If it is against the will of God for a man to lie with a man, it is also against His for a woman to lie with a woman.

To prevent a debate on the issue, we have provided proof written in the book of Romans, Chapter 1. This is what it says, "For this cause God gave them over to vile affections: for even their women did change the natural use into that which is against nature" (v. 26). The verse tells us that the women deviated from the natural way. A woman having sexual attraction for a man is the natural way. Therefore, the unnatural way is a woman having sexual attraction for a woman. God also refers to it as vile affections in the same verse. Verse 27 reveals to us that the men no longer desired sex with women. Instead, they engaged in sexual intercourse with one another. Homosexuality is whether two women or two men is considered unnatural and abominable (Leviticus 20:13, 15-16).

When something is abominable or an abomination in the sight of God, it means that God has a strong hate toward it. He is disgusted by it and sees it as a terrible thing to do, and He still does, today. God changes not. According to what is written He is the same today, yesterday, and forever (Hebrews 13:8). There is more evidence that same sex is sexual sin written in 1 Corinthians. It is there that we are told that the unrighteous shall not inherit the kingdom of God (v. 6:9). We are also given a list of sins to clarify certain forms of unrighteousness. Among what is listed, we find the word effeminate. If it's wrong for men to behave like a feminine woman, it is also wrong for a woman to behave like a masculine man. This also means that men should not be wearing clothing associated with women, and women should not be wearing clothing associated with men. Deuteronomy 22:5 says it this way, "The woman shall not wear that which pertaineth unto a man, neither shall a man put on a woman's garment: for all that do so are abomination unto the Lord thy God." You can also see that God views such a person as an abomination; He strongly dislikes what they do because it is unnatural behavior. Well, if a man is not permitted to act like a woman and if a woman can't act like a man, what does that tell us about same sex relationships?

1 Corinthians 6:9 also gives us the words, "abusers of themselves with mankind." Indeed, women can accomplish sex with one another, but they can't abuse one another like men can. This is because women do not have the ability to penetrate one another. Paul referred to what the men were doing with one another indecent (Romans 1:27) However, in verse 27, the same thing is not said in reference to the women. Men do not have vaginas. Therefore, when two men engage in sex, one penetrates the anus of the other, which

is how men potentially abuse one another. This is due to the inability of the penetrated area to naturally lubricate or expand. There is never a time that a man can justify inserting his penis in another man for sexual pleasure because it ought not ever be done. Jesus speaks of what we call the anus as the draught, the place where waste exits the body (Matthew 15:17).

If a person understands love they should also know that there is nothing abusive about love. Don't be deceived by the "love is love" statement that many who choose to be gay use to try to justify same sex relationships. True love is determined by God, who is love. As our creator, we can love no one more than we love Him, not even ourselves (Matthew 10:37; 22:37; Exodus 20:3). To disobey God's will for sexuality is not love. It is evil in His sight. Therefore, if we call what God hates love, we are guilty of rebelling against God. Hate is the reason we have effeminate and same sex today just as it was in the days of Lot and Noah. Just like the cities of Sodom and Gomorrah approved of the same sex lifestyle, the same lifestyle is legal and also celebrated in the United States. The LGBTIQ community as they are called today, even have a month dedicated to them, called, the "pride month." Regardless of how right the world makes the lifestyle out to be, God changes not, and He will someday judge the disobedient. We can also be sure that if the men mentioned in Romans 1:27 suffered a due penalty within themselves, there are many today, who are suffering physically and mentally, too. There are many sicknesses and diseases associated with sexual sin. Paul made this known to us in 1 Corinthians 6:18. He tells us that people who practice sexual sin, sin against their own body. This is another reason why repentance is necessary and encouraged. There is no escaping the suffering for sexual sin. The suffering also is necessary for the sake of deterring people from sexual immorality. Unfortunately, not even the things people suffer because of disobedience, will lead everyone to repentance.

At some point in life, we become of age where we know right

from wrong. When a child gets to the point in their life that their parents' discipline doesn't break them or when we get to that age where we make decisions for ourselves, it is at the point that we can hear the truth and do what is right to do. Cain and Abel had to offer unto God a sacrifice when they became of age. They were not ignorant of the truth. However, one offered a sacrifice that was according to the will of God and the other offered what he wanted to. God accepted the right sacrifice and rejected the one that was offered in conflict to the will of God. Cain wasn't ignorant to the truth. He deliberately rebelled against the will of God. Most of the LGBTIQ community are not ignorant to the truth. Rather they are just like Cain; they are rebelling against the truth. We all have a conscience built inside of us. We also have a God who is all-knowing. He knows the thoughts and intent of the heart. He is aware of who is ignorant and who is not. If what we do is pleasing in the sight of God, there'll be no feeling of guilt and it will not bother us if others know that we do it. Unfortunately, those who love darkness rather than light, want to keep what they do in the dark. They love what they do but just don't want others to know about what they do. If others know about it, they don't want anyone to call what they do, displeasing in the sight of God. Perhaps this is why Jesus said, "And this is the condemnation, that light has come into the world, and men loved darkness rather than light, because their deeds were evil" (John 3:19).

The light exposes what people do in the dark. Jesus goes further to say in verse 20, "For everyone that doeth evil hates the light, neither cometh to the light, lest his deeds should be reproved." The legalization of same sex marriage has given some the impression that same sex has been made right. However, God is greater than man and the laws man implement to approve sinful lifestyles. The message of love is viewed by many of the LGBTIQ community as a message of hate only because it bothers them when their evil deeds are exposed. However, if evil is not exposed we would all get what we deserve. Thankfully God doesn't desire anyone to perish, and therefore, He delivers to us the truth that saves all who believe. We, who serve God, tell others the same message of love that we heard and believed, that others might have the same opportunity granted to us. However, those who hate the light, want to force those who have come to the light, to accept their lifestyle as something good although they know God hates what they do. The truth is, many people in the world will hear the truth and although some will hear and believe, many will hear and refuse to believe. What's most important is that the children of God do the will of God and speak the truth. If we don't, the blood of many shall be on our hands. Jesus is the first to reveal to the truth the world. Although He exposed us all guilty of sin, He also made it known that His reason for coming into the world wasn't to condemn anyone, but that the world through Him might be saved (John 3:17). Therefore, let it be known that it is the will of God that those who follow in His footsteps tell others the truth from above. We do it for the same reason the Lord Himself did it; we love you and do not want anyone to perish. In the next chapter, we will deal with the issue of masturbation, which is another immoral practice that is often done in the dark.

CHAPTER 4
Guilty of Sexual Sin Without a Sex Partner

The rabbit hole of sexual sin is very broad; there are various immoral ways that people in the world sexually please themselves. The boundary that God put in place within the human race, doesn't just cover same sex. Sexual pleasure is often accomplished without the aid of anyone. Therefore, it is important I expose the one sexual immoral act that is not often talked about. There are many in the world using different methods to sexually satisfy themselves. The will of God is absolutely no sexual pleasure until marriage. Adam was obviously a virgin until he was joined as husband and wife with Eve. When I speak of a virgin, I am speaking of a person who has never had sex. We must not assume that just because a person appears not interested in a mate of the opposite sex, doesn't mean that he or she is not receiving sexual pleasure. Fornication is not simply two people having sex together before marriage. It is any form of sexual pleasure prior to marriage. The goal of sex is to reach a climax, to get to the point where ejaculation happens and/or an orgasm occurs. Penis to vagina is not the only way that this is achieved. There is also oral sex which is mouth to vagina or mouth to penis. However, when a person is satisfying themselves they use something that is a part of themselves, such as a finger. Otherwise, they use one of man's evil inventions that are specifically made for a person who wants to satisfy themselves.

People who sexually satisfy themselves know that what they do is wrong whether they know what God thinks about it or not. This act is also kept a secret. It is also something that Satan has influenced many young people to do. Those who satisfy themselves are simply substituting the way it was meant to be done, with an alternate way that doesn't require the participation of someone else. Perhaps some do it because they perceive it to be safer than having sex with other people. Regardless of the reason, God wants people to know that it is sexual sin and ought not be done by anyone. No matter what Satan tells you, it is not natural for us to sexually satisfy ourselves, and none of us would have ever done it if we weren't influenced to do it. Just like homosexuality and bestiality, it too, is learned behavior. Please understand that Satan specializes in tricking people to do what is against God. He is recognized by Jesus as the father of lies (John 8:44). This is not something that he just started doing. He's been lying from the very beginning of human existence. "Woe to them that call evil good, and good evil; that put darkness for light, and light for darkness; that put bitter for sweet, and sweet for bitter" (Isaiah 5:20). Who do you think deceive people to call evil good and good evil! It is the father of lies and he has caused many to depart from the faith. He is not to be given any place.

The evil one's philosophy is, "why depend on someone else to achieve sexual satisfaction when you can do things to sexually satisfy yourself!" The nature of Satan is revealed to us first, in the book of Genesis, chapter 3. It is there that Satan took the truth and turned it around as the lie and the lie and turned it around as the truth. We also know that there are 3 ways that Satan tempts us: The lust of the flesh, the lust of the eyes, and pride of life (1 John 2:16). When Satan deceived Eve, she saw the forbidden fruit as good for food, appealing to the eye, and a way to become wise (Genesis 3:6). This tells me that people become curious about masturbation after hearing about it from others or seeing it demonstrated in movies or described in books. Perhaps I should also include social media as one the ways evil is influenced. If Eve had not given ear to Satan's lie, she would have never even considered eating from the forbidden tree. Satan uses the same tactic on all people and many get comfortable with doing things what we ought not. According to what is written, "the imagination of a man's heart is evil from his youth" (Genesis 8:21). This reveals that Satan began influencing a person's life as early as childhood. Therefore, it is important that the eyes and ears of our children are guarded. Anybody who began masturbating at an early age can bear witness to how addictive it. Many youths and adults are enslaved by such a practice. However, it is important that people know whether they do it or not, that such a practice is evil. It is after we know what the truth is that we can no longer do what is right to do ignorant to what God thinks about. It's like James wrote, "to them who know what is right to do and they do it, to them it is sin" (James 4:17). Our knowledge of the truth makes us accountable. Although Satan has blinded the mind of many who take pleasure in unrighteousness, you do not have to fall into the same category (2 Corinthians 4:4). You can hear and believe. It is my goal to encourage you to seek God for deliverance from self satisfying yourself. I can bear witness to the stronghold of it. I was once where many are today. It was something that I practiced for many years of my life being ignorant to the truth that it wasn't just something that people shouldn't do, but that is also something God hates. Thankfully I can say, I am delivered from it by the power of God. You can also be delivered. Don't be like those who have a form of godliness but deny the power of God to operate in their life. I can assure that those who truly believe, will not continue the practice of sin. God has made his word simple for us to understand. According to 1 John 3:8, the people who practice sin are of the devil. That is how we all started out. The same verse reveals to us that it is because of sin that the Son of God came that He might destroy the works of the devil. Because came into the world, the world through Him can be saved (John 3:17). In chapter 5, we will talk about the many ways people are groomed by others into a sexually immoral lifestyle as early as childhood to be sexually immoral.

CHAPTER 5
Sexual Immorality is Influenced as Early as Childhood

Those who were fortunate to be raised by godly parents are blessed to receive knowledge, wisdom, and understanding of God very earlier in life (Proverbs 22:6). Some have actually been taught the importance of loving someone first, and when they're older enough get married. It is instilled in them that marriage is until death do apart and that the marriage bedroom is the approved place to enjoy the fruit of sex with their lover. Unfortunately, many of us were not privileged to be raised in a Christian home. We did not witness our parents praying and reading the bible. They never told us what things the Lord hates or that we should save ourselves until married. We had no clue that there was a way of the Lord. I'm sure it wasn't their intention to teach us to do sinful things, but many of us learned to do evil by watching our parents and other relatives and friends. Whether we were taught to be sexually immoral or not, we can be certain that the various sexual immoral practices have the tendency to be learned by some of us as early as childhood (Genesis 8:21). We've seen it with our own eyes or we've had unwelcome experiences against our will (Matthew 18:9). You've heard the saying, "The apple doesn't fall too far from the tree," haven't you? Perhaps you have also heard the familiar saying, "Like father, like son," or "like mother, like daughter." Such sayings are so true. The children tend to become like their parents and/or other relatives and friends that they grew up around. As a result, we were like "monkey see, monkey do. It is normal for children to grow up imitating what their eyes were allowed to see.

For example, it's not by coincidence that every male in some families as far back as great, great, great, granddaddy, has committed a crime, been incarcerated, got more than one baby momma, is known for alcoholism, known for using drugs, for being verbally, physically, or sexually abusive, known for committed adultery, etc. Many parents and/or grandparents still ask their sons or daughters, who the parents or grandparents are of the person they have taken interest in. They use the information given to them to determine whether the person's character is good or evil. This is because a child cannot be raised to be any different from those who raised them. Indeed, it is good for us who are now in the body of Christ, to also know who our children are hanging out or spending time with. Just because we are teaching our children the way of the Lord, it doesn't mean that they are not curious about sin and sex in particular. They are also influenced by the world and may very well see nothing wrong with conforming to it.

However, what you'll never see is a parent living in sin raising their children up in the way of the Lord. This is because they can't do it. Teaching requires the person teaching to lead by example. One thing is for sure, the blind cannot lead the blind (Luke 6:39-49). Neither a person with the log in their eye, as Jesus puts it, can see clearly to get the speck out of someone else's eye (Matthew 7:3-5),. Even if a drinking father or smoking mother tells their children not to smoke or drink, the child might not do it while still a child but when they're older, they too, will seek to do the same. My point is, preaching "don't do this or that" is a waste of time, if the person preaching fails to exemplify what they say is right to do. A sexually immoral influences sexual immorality because that is what others see them engaging in.

Ultimately, the sin or evil people do is nothing more than a curse that continues from generation to generation. The curse of sin goes all the way back to the very first man to disobey God. We were all created by one blood, the first man known to us as Adam (Acts 17:26). Death came as the result of his disobedience that now affects all people (Romans 5:15). All of us at some point in life are eventually guilty of sin (Romans 3.23; 1 John 1:10). The curse of sin which our Lord died to take away is broken in the life of every person who hears and believes the word of God unto a changed life (Galatians 3:13). When we die to the desires of the flesh and live unto God after the seed of Christ takes root in our heart, we become new creatures, who exemplify righteousness (2 Corinthians 5:17). John says it another way! He said, "Whosoever is born of God doth not commit sin; for his seed remaineth in him: he cannot sin, because he is born of God" (v. 9, KJV).

Once a person is new, they can and will teach others to do what is right in the sight of God and make themselves as the example to follow, just as Christ is the example that all believers must imitate (Matthew 5:16; Ephesians 5:1). It is expected for the righteous to train up our children to follow our example as we follow Christ. We have to teach our children what sexual sin is and that God hates it. We must not leave one stone unturned. They need to know that sexually satisfying themselves is sin also. We also have to expose the consequences that are the outcome of having sex outside of marriage. Then a visual picture of what is right to do must be exemplified in their presences. They must see their parents be faithful to one, avoiding sexually explicit music, books, and movies. It is a blessing for a child to be trained up in the way of the Lord!

Before I became a new creature in Christ, I was a drunkard and sexually immoral just like my daddy, but my old lifestyle, none of my children have been exposed to. Instead, they have been taught to serve the Lord and to follow my example as I follow Christ. When we see children and/or people being sexual immoral, we don't need to ask ourselves the question, "why do they do what they do," if we understand that people learn to do what they do from watching others, and that home is the primary place where evil influence, we'll not have to be shocked when see our youth being sexually immoral. The devil doesn't wait for a child to become an adult to plant the seed. The younger the better as far as he's concerned.

Children will not only do what they see others do, many children are taken advantage of. They are used for sexual gratification by those adults that have frequent access to them. Children have been forced to watch pornography, They have been forced to participate in sex. They have been fondled and other things as a tactic used to groom them. All such grooming is against their will and is kept secret by the sexual predators who violate them. The youth are vulnerable, easily influenced and easily taken advantage of. I was a young man when I experienced sex for the first time. I can remember it like yesterday after all these years. The woman lived not too far from my childhood home. I think I might have been fifteen or sixteen years old at the time, but I'm not sure. All I know is I was in high school.

During the summer she would pay me to cut the grass. One day she asked me to come to her house while her husband was away. Out of curiosity I did what she asked. I was already curious about what it's like to have sex with someone. Perhaps Proverbs 7:18-19 says it all: Come, let us take our fill of love until the morning: let us solace ourselves with love." Yes, I was an unwise young man with no one to show me the right way. My experience with her was far too much for a person my age. Not only did it increase my desire for more of the same, but I had become a sex crazed individual. I couldn't get enough of what I felt that night, and it led to me longing for that experience over, and over again.

I became addicted to masturbation and fornication, both, and as I mentioned earlier, an addiction to porn would soon follow. I wanted sex as often as possible. I was in spiritual bondage without a clue of what that really was at the time. So, from my own experience, I understand why sex has its appropriate time and place, and if experienced too soon it can ruin a young person's life. The young mind is not mentally prepared for sexual experience. All it takes is a little grooming when we're too young to process it all and the seed of sin is successfully planted.

A young person might even think that he or she is ready to experience sex in their mind or that they are mature enough for it, but none really are. May the Lord protect our children from sexual predators, who take advantage of the youth for the sake of sexual pleasure. There is never a time when adults have the right to use a child for sexual pleasure, even if the child appears to be a willing participant. You'll be surprised who is a sexual predator! There is the neighbor, a parent, a relative, a politician, religious leader, teacher, coach, and the list goes on, who have sexually taken advantage of children of various ages. Sex with children has caused many to lose their jobs, their licenses or practice, ended up with a bad reputation, and been incarcerated, millions of dollars, etc. Absolutely, no one can be trusted to be alone with our children alone. Godly parents, we must use wisdom and do all we can to protect our children from sexual predators.

"Woe to them," who used children for sexual gratification or exposed them to sexual immorality! A person who causes a child to stumble by what they expose them to is better off committing suicide, or as the word of God says it, "better of tying a millstone upon their neck and sinking to the depths of the sea" (Luke 17:2, KJV). The worse a person could ever do is influence a person to think that evil is good. Especially a child. If God says that a person is better off dead, it will also mean that he or she shall not inherit the kingdom of God if they fail to repent.

Children who are sexually violated do not qualify as willing participants, nor do they know and understand the truth. Therefore, they are not held accountable for what the sexually immoral do to them. However, children do not remain children forever but eventually reach the age where they can utilize their freewill. Once they know better they are held accountable for what they choose. God protected the children that live to see adult age. No one survives childhood trauma with God. Unfortunately, it is when a child becomes an adult that the sexual things they experienced in their youth become a willing lifestyle for many of them. In other words, the very thing they hated being done to them when they were children, and the things that they curiously experienced although they were not mentally prepared for, they choose to do as adults. So, many who were molested or raped, or who experienced sex in their youth often become promiscuous engaging in fornication (including incest), bestiality, homosexuality, and adultery as adults. Many of them do unto others what was done unto them.

The good thing about them growing into adulthood is, they then know right from wrong. At that point, they can then hear the truth and decide for themselves whether to believe or not. We were all shown mercy during a period of our life, but the time comes, when God no longer accepts being ignorant of the truth as an excuse. He makes sure that the truth reaches our ears and that we truly understand His will. Repentance is the responsibility of the hearer (Romans 10:17). None of us can use our childhood experiences as an excuse to be sexually immoral because the same God who allowed us to experience it in our youth has the power to break the curse over our life when we are old enough to choose to do His will.

It is God's will that all become new creatures, which are born of God. The old sexually immoral creatures that existed until we heard the truth, must pass away (1 Corinthians 5:17; Romans 6:2). So, if you have been molested and/or raped during your childhood, know that God is your hope for a better life. Jesus died for all people, not some, including you (John 3:16). This is because at some point in life, we are all guilty of doing what God hates. I'm sure you longed for God to punish those who violated you in your youth, and if you believe that they deserve to be punished, you must also know that you too, deserve to be punished if you refuse to hear the truth and believe. None of us can cast the first stone because we have all sinned and come short of the glory of God.

Please understand that a rapist or molester is no different than a fornicator, and an adulterer, or any other sexually immoral person. It all falls into the category of sexual sin. Don't let your childhood experience cause you to hate God unto the damning of your soul. You made it to adulthood because God was with you in the storm of your life, and He is the only reason you were able to endure all you went through.

Many people lock their traumatic experiences away in their mind which is not the right thing to do. We must learn to forgive those who violated us so that we don't go our entire life bitter and filled with hate and blocking out the voice of God. You are no longer a victim. Hear the truth and let the truth set you free. Chapter 6 will discuss the topic of incest. We have already proved that many or molested and raped during their childhood. Therefore, it is not difficult to understand that the many people guilty of incest.

CHAPTER 6
The Sexually Forbidden Person of the Opposite Sex

So far, we've exposed a lot of sexual immorality but there is more that we need to take into consideration. No, we can't satisfy ourselves sexually. Yes, same sex intercourse is sin. Sex with animals is sin, but also that people acknowledge that sex with certain relatives is forbidden, too. Indeed, sexual intercourse is intended to be enjoyed between a man and a woman only, but a person should never consider having sexual intercourse with anyone that they are a parent or guardian (includes uncle and aunt) to, or a sibling to. Some would probably say at this point, "As long as they're blood related to me." However, the word of God proves a statement to one's opinion only. The word of God is the foundation of truth and what God says, goes. Jesus told us that a man shall live by every word that proceeded out of the mouth of God (Matthew 4:4). The truth can't be individually determined. It must be the same for the entire human race. If not, someone can justify incest. Some could say that you don't have to be married to have sex. Someone could say, it doesn't matter if your spouse is human, is the same sex, is nonhuman, is a child, is our own child, is our parent, etc. Ultimately, it would also mean that we do not have a God that we have to answer to. Order is necessary! Otherwise, the establishment of government is meaningless. Fortunately, there is a God and the word of God is a life unto our feet, a lamp unto our path (Psalms 119:105).

Written in the word of is the order of relationship. The reason it is available to us is because God is against sexual sin, including incest. Now, I want to direct your attention to the book of Leviticus, which was delivered unto the people after they were brought out of slavery down in Egypt. It is safe to say that there were such things going on in the earth that God did not want his people to commit.

One of the first thing God does is deal with sexual relations. Leviticus, chapter 20 and verse 11 says, "And the man that lieth with his father's wife hath uncovered his father's wife hath uncovered his nakedness: both of them shall surely be put to death; their blood shall be upon them."

I'm sure that the first thing that comes to a person's mind when they read the verse I quoted is, the verse is talking about a man having a relationship with his own biological mother. Indeed, that is incest, but a man's father's wife doesn't have to his blood mother. She could also be stepmother or mother by marriage or shall I say, by law.. Not only would she be considered his mother, she would still be off limits because she is his father's wife. Verse 11 is proof that both blood related and certain individuals married into the family or off limits. A child can be influenced to do sexually forbidden things and not know any better. An adult, on the other hand, should know that he or she cannot get involved with a parent or guardian, or with a sibling whether blood related or such by marriage. s right from wrong, and no adult child can justify having a sexual attraction toward their parent or guardian whether biological or by law. This also includes those who adopt children. How can it be OK for a person to marry a person who has children whom they are supposed to be a mother or father to, justify being sexually involved with the children under their parental guidance! How can a child refer to a person as their mother or father if their mother or father is involved with them sexually. The title mother, father, mother-n-law, father-n-law, sibling or step sister comes with responsibility. Let me also not fail to mention the title uncle or aunt. If the titles don't mean anything, what is the purpose of their existence! Because they exist, we know God expects for those who are such to act accordingly. I want to encourage you to read Leviticus, chapter 20 and Deuteronomy 20:20-23. To make it even clearer that incest is a big deal in the sight of God, we are given a good example of this in Paul's first letter to the Corinthians. It is in chapter 5 where we read about a man involved with his father's wife (5:1). The woman was more than likely the man's stepmother. At the time, such a relationship was not even something that was common among the gentiles (unbelievers). Paul addresses the issue because the man was accepted by the body of believers, who was aware that the woman was the man's father's wife, which makes her his mother by either blood or by law.

This also reveals that believers should not ignore sinful acts committed within the body of Christ. Indeed, what the man was guilty of, was sin because Paul calls it fornication in the first verse. Incest is just another form of fornication, which is nothing more that having sex with someone you're not married to. No man can marry his own mother whether biological or stepmother. Paul's statement, "deliver such an one unto Satan for the destruction of the flesh, that the spirit may be saved in the day of the Lord Jesus (v. 5) tells us that the matter was serious. No one should be given the impression that the sin they do is not that serious. All sin is serious in the sight of God, and all who refuse to stop sinning He will judge. Paul wasn't giving the people his opinion but he made sure that they knew that he was speaking as a representative of the Lord, Jesus Christ (v. 4). Lastly, if Paul hadn't dealt with the issue, the man's sinful practice would have become the sinful practices of others in the group. This too, Paul makes known unto us in verse 6 and 7. Incest will continue to spread throughout the generations of a family, if the word of God bring about a change. Jesus tells us that the word of God is the only power that can put an end to a sin altogether. According to what is written in the book of Matthews, the word causes conflict between members of the family. Jesus said, "Think not that I am come to bring peace. I did not come bring peace, but a sword instead" (v. 34). The sword that Jesus is referring to is the word. When the truth is heard by a family, some in the family will hear and believe and some will not believe. This will lead to a conflict between individuals. "For I have come to set a man at variance against his father, and the daughter against her mother, and the daughter-n-law against her mother-n-law'(v. 35). Those who believe within the family die to sin and practice sin no longer. They will know that having sex with mother, father, sister, brother, aunt, and uncle, including step parents and step siblings is fornication. They will flee it as Paul commanded in 1 Corinthians 6:9. The same will expose family members to be guilty of sexual sin. Lastly, when a person who experienced incest become parents to children, they will train their own children up in the way of the Lord as Proverbs 22:6 says.

Those who are caught up in forbidden sexual relationships are consciously aware that what they are doing is not good to do because they do it in secret. Some work extremely hard at keeping it from being exposed publicly. Furthermore, in most societies there is laws against incest. Many daughters end up pregnant by their biological father or stepfathers. In the United States, when the blood reveals who the father is, he is arrested and incarcerated. It is considered a sexual offense and when the man is released from prison, he is put on a lifetime registry and identified as a sex offender. So, as you can see, even the law agrees with the word of God on some things. We can be confident that sexual predators are not ignorant of the law. In conclusion, ONLY THE HUSBAND AND WIFE of each family has the God given right to enjoy sex with one another. In Chapter 7, we will deal with promiscuity and some of the consequences that the promiscuous suffer.

CHAPTER 7
Promiscuity is Sexually Immoral

Be fruitful and multiply and fill the earth," must not be taken out of context. It must not be used as a justification for a person to engage in sex with multiple people. Having children is only good when it is done in obedience to God. When a person engages in sexual intercourse with multiple individuals, they are becoming one in a sense with every person they sleep with. Jesus reveals this to us in the conversation that he had with the Samaritan while at the well. He proved the woman guilty of sexual immorality. He told her, "Go, call your husband, and the two of you come back" (John 4:16). Surely, Jesus whether or not the woman had a husband. However, His reason for telling her to go get her husband was to expose her sin. This is what the word does and Jesus as the Son of God was the word in human form (John 1:14). Therefore, every word that proceeded out of His mouth was according to the truth (Matthew 4:4). It was the word of God. The word of God has no effect if it is not heard. Faith comes by hearing it (Romans 10:17). So, Jesus needed for the woman to hear the word that she might have the opportunity to believe. The woman's response to what Jesus said was, "I don't have a husband." The woman was claiming that she wasn't married. Now, if she was married, she couldn't possibly have a husband, and if no husband, she shouldn't be sexually involved with anyone. However, after she told Jesus that she had no husband, Jesus agreed with her, but not agreed with her. Let me explain! Lawfully, the Samaritan woman was indeed single, but spiritually, she had been joined as one with others. Jesus told her this, "Thou hast well said, I have no husband: For thou hast had five husbands; and he whom thou now hast is not thy husband: in that sadist thou truly" (v. 17-18).

According to what Jesus said, she had not been legally married to anyone, but spiritually married to five men, and unlawfully involved with someone who is married to someone else. Jesus is teaching us that sexual intercourse with a person joins us to them, and God would not have us joined to anyone we're not married to or anyone who is already married to someone else. To make it plain, fornication and adultery is sin. In the sight of a promiscuous is irresponsible. They have a desire for sexual pleasure but they do not want the responsibility that comes with marriage. Such a lifestyle is dangerous. The problem with it is, it is a sin against one's own body (Roman 1:27; 1 Corinthians 6:18). Just how dangerous it! It so dangerous that Paul writes, "Flee fornication and goes further to tell us why. When a person sins against their own body, it means that their sowing of sexual immorality results in them reaping consequences for their disobedience. Solomon asked a question in the book of Proverbs, chapter 6. He said, "Can a man take fire in his bosom and his clothes not be burned" (v. 27). Surely there is nothing good about fire in a person's bosom. If fire touches any part of our body, it will cause us pain. The pain will cause us unwanted discomfort. Therefore, it is wise for us to be celibate until we get married. It is especially wise that we avoid promiscuity. Verse 26 of the same chapter speaks of the outcome of a man getting involved with a whorish woman. The word, whorish simply implies a person who sleeps around just like the word, promiscuity does. Although it is used by Solomon in reference to a woman, it also applies to a man. What Solomon is trying to us is, if a person is promiscuous or sleeping with someone they're not married to, there is a good chance that they are carriers of disease. The words, "brought to a piece of bread," makes me think of a decline in health. This confirms what Paul already told us. Sleeping around has been the downfall of many people. Many men have had exactly what Solomon said in Proverbs, Chapter 7 to happen to them. He writes, "For she hath cast down many wounded: yea, many strong men have been slain by her" (v. 26). Notice it says, "many men!" This is a sure indication that the woman had been with many men, which means she was a promiscuous woman. Again, men also fall into the same category as the woman mentioned in the passage, and many women's lives have been ruined after sleeping with promiscuous men. I'm only trying to show just how dangerous the promiscuous lifestyle is. Verse 22 speaks of the danger of the lifestyle also by saying, "He goes after her straightway, as an ox goes to the slaughter, or a fool to the correction of the stock. Then, verse 23 says, "Till a dart strikes through his liver as a bird haste to the snare and knows not that it is for his life." Because many choose to disobey the will of God having knowledge of the truth and the eternal consequences, there are various sicknesses and diseases that the promiscuous suffer which also serve as signs that God hates what they do.

Also, promiscuity is the cause of many children coming into the world having to live in single parent homes. If it took two people to achieve procreation, it also takes two to take on the responsibility of raising and providing for the child(ren). Children need both of their parents in their lives. At least, until they are old enough to make it in life without. Can a man and a woman provide good parenting living in separate homes? If they can, fornication is good, not evil. The truth is, good will never come out of doing evil. The child(ren) will be affected by the absence of their mother or father. Therefore, the father and the mother are intended to live in the same household as husband and wife (Genesis 2:24; Ephesians 5:22-23). Well, if a man has many children by many different women, it is impossible for him to be the head of multiple households.

Also, the parents that don't live with their children tend to be strangers to them. Especially, if he or she doesn't live within close proximity. Most people facilitate frequent visits with their outside children from out of state, or out of the country. The most that many outside parents can do is, support their offspring financially and have visits with them from time to time. However, it would be impossible for a man or woman to be the kind of parent God created us to be. In most cases, men who have multiple children by multiple women struggle financially because they are obligated to support their children financially by law. Perhaps this is part of what Proverbs 5:10 is saying, "Lest strangers be filled with thy wealth; and thy labors be in the house of a stranger." debt is indeed one of the consequences for sexual sin. I know this from experience! Sexual pleasure with someone you're not married to is "all good" until a baby comes into the picture. Paying child support, having visitation with my son while trying to be a husband to my wife and a father to our son, was overwhelming. For years I had to endure financial strain.

It is not the will of God that any of us lack what we need or suffer financial strain. However, He is not to blame for what we suffer; disobedience is. Debt is self-inflicted. We bring it upon ourselves. If we obey God, do what He says, we shall not lack what is necessary for us to have (Matthew 625-33; 1 Thessalonians 4:11-12; Hebrews 13:5). Having children with people you're not married to is never to be perceived as a blessing under no circumstance. What we do is either good or it's evil. It's either right or it's not. It's either according to the truth or the lie. In chapter 8, we will go into depth about why marriage is the one relationship that is honorable in God's sight.

CHAPTER 8
Only Marriage is Honorable in the Sight of God

There is only one way to avoid the consequences that follow sexual sin. That one way is marriage. From the very beginning, we are told that a man is to leave his parents and be cleave to his wife (Genesis 2:24). A woman is a gift that God desires for a man to have. We know this because it was God who said that it wasn't good for man to be alone (v. 18). Every man that desires marriage wants his wife to himself. The wife is not simply just some woman; she is bone of the man's bone and the flesh of his flesh. The two of them are one (v. 23). The woman as a blessing to man is also revealed to us in the book of Proverbs. There we are told that when a man finds a woman he finds a thing, and she is a blessing from the Lord (18:22). When a man is ready for a wife, is it at that point that he is already for sex. In Paul's letter, he tells us two things: 1) flee fornication and 2) get married to avoid it (1 Corinthians 6:18; 7:1). Paul then tells us the right thing to do. He says, "Let every man have his own wife, and let every woman have her own husband" (7:2). A man's wife is his and no one else. Likewise, he is hers and no one else. The only person they're supposed to desire sex with is one another. Indeed, a woman is the man's gift, but marriage is not simply all about the man. It is for women also. Many women are guilty of fornication just as many men. Therefore, women need to have their own man just as many men need their own woman, too. When it comes to sex the man doesn't call the shots, either. In other words, he doesn't decide when he and his wife will have sex. Verse 4 says, "The wife hath not power of her own body, but the husband; and likewise, also the husband hath not power of his own body, but the wife. If this is understood by them, they will not keep sex from one another. Besides sex is a very important part of marriage. In fact, a desire for sex makes marriage necessary. Sex is so important that if a married person is deprived of it for a long period of time, it can lead to vulnerability. Satan will use the long break from sex as an opportunity to tempt the one in need for it. This is why Paul says, "Defraud ye not one the other, except it be with consent for a time (a short period), that ye may give yourselves to fasting and prayer; and come together again, that Satan tempt you not for your incontinency" (v. 5). As you can see, Satan doesn't want people to be married unto the glory of God. Therefore, he seized the opportunity to cause the husband or wife to commit adultery. However, if both the husband and wife are in the will of God, they will not intentionally deny one another sexual satisfaction. Instead they will enjoy the fruit thereof. Chapter 9 will deal with how many people a man or a woman can be married to at once.

CHAPTER 9
In the Body of Christ, Polygamy Is Sexual Immoral

This brings me to the issue of polygamy! We also have those who try to get around the marriage license so that they can justify being married to more than one woman, particularly in America. This is because it is against the law for a man to be married to more than one woman at a time. The government has a record of every legal marriage in the United States. If a man attempts to take another wife while is still legally married, if caught, he would be guilty of bigamy. For part, bigamists keep the woman he attempts to marry from his legal wife. This within itself tells us that the man knows that it is not right to do. Involvement with her is considered adultery in the sight of God. God gave unto Adam one female companion for a wife. A man guilty of bigamy doesn't leave his first wife. Instead, he lives a double life. He juggles between two women who live in two different places without either of the two knowing about one another. Technically, the only way a man can get away with having more than one wife in America is to do it illegally.

Unfortunately, many religious groups who do follow the teachings of Jesus Christ pervert the word of God to justify a man having more than one wife. What we know from what is written in the word of God, the marriage of every man of God that we read about is recognized and honored by God. A man and his wife were also recognized as such by the community. The desire for more than one wife has nothing to do with love, Having more than one simply gives a sexually immoral man more access to unlimited sexual pleasure. What is the difference between a man having multiple illegal wives that he engages in sex with and a man that simply enjoys sex with multiple women. There is no difference.

If it's fornication when a person sleeps with one or more people that they're not married to, it is still fornication when a man sleeps with multiple women that he is not legally married to although he claims them to be his wives. We can't simply take a man's word for it, because a man who doesn't walk in obedience to the Lord, will only do what seems right to him and expect it to be accepted by everyone else. Since marriage is founded by God, the standard of marriage is also set by God. The word of God is the only authority, and it is the same today, yesterday, and forever, and it applies the same to all of mankind. Any religious group who believes in polygamy is not founded on the word of God. Let us consider the human body. Everything comes in two is assigned to either the left or the right of us. We have two working unitedly together. Can you imagine us having more than two arms! What would be your reaction if you saw a person with more than two! You would not think that they're normal. Is it by coincidence that God only gave Adam one wife or that he created us male and female.

The word of God tells us to try every spirit to see if that spirit is of God (1 John 4:1). It goes further to tell us why. It says because many false prophets have gone out into the world. Well, what do false prophets do! They pervert the truth to gain their own following (Acts 20:29-30). In verse 30, Paul reveals what false prophets do. He said they speak perverse things, to draw away disciples after them. My point is, The truth applies to the entire human race. Therefore, there can only be one true teaching concerning marriage. All other doctrines are founded by seducing spirit and doctrines of demons as Paul calls them in 1 Timothy 4:1. So, based on what the word of God says, cover to cover, where does the Lord speak from his mouth that man can have more than one wife in the body of Christ. He didn't say it anywhere. Also, all the teaching by the apostles speaks of marriage between one man and one woman. Paul specifically says, "let every man have his own wife and let every woman have her own husband" (1 Corinthians 7:2). From this we know that a single spouse is the will of God. The Lord's church is also spoken of in the singular. The church is His one bride (Ephesians 5:25). When the truth is perverted something added to or taken from it, which is what is being done to keep people from doing the will of God.

Perhaps, polygamy is legal in certain countries. It means nothing if it goes against the truth of the word of God. What God says overrides all laws and all governments. There's an old saying, "It takes two to tangle." Well, how many people does it take to reproduce? It only takes two and just as a man has a lot of sperm, one wife can get pregnant multiple times, and the two of them can sexually satisfy one another over, and over again. Therefore, there is no need for more than one woman to be joined to one man. If Jesus said, "what God has joined together, let no man divide," how many people is he referring to? Is it not two, one male and one female. Do any of us have more than one biological father and mother?

Furthermore, a man has one penis for a reason, just as a woman has one vagina for a reason. If it's OK for the man's penis to entertain more than one vagina, it would also have to be OK for a woman's vagina to entertain multiple penises. I am purposely sounding like a fool so you can see how the concept of a man having multiple wives has sexual immorality written all over it. Let's face it! Polygamy whether legally or illegally practiced is not holy and acceptable in the sight of God.

Furthermore, it is impossible for one man to love more than one woman the same. He will automatically love the one more than he loves all others. He will spend more time with one and do more for one than the others. We can learn this truth from Jacob's experience with Leah and Rachel, and Elkanah's experience with his wives Peninnah and Hannah. Both Jacob and Elkanah loved one wife more than they did the other (1 Genesis 29:17-18; Samuel 1:4-5) A man can only give his heart to one woman at a time. It's just like our relationship with God. We can't love anything or anybody on the same level that we love Him. Neither can we say we love Him if we love something or someone more than we love Him. Either God is our Master, the one whom we serve, or our heart is filled with something or someone other than Him, which means we do not honor Him as the authority in our lives (Matthew 6:24; Romans 6:16).

It was Jesus our Lord who taught that a person cannot serve two masters. He emphasized that a person favors one over the other, that they would cling to only one and not them both. We are the bride of Christ and His only, and we are expected to be faithful to Him and not go whoring with the world. Likewise, just as the Lord has ONE church or bride, a man can also only have ONE wife. Furthermore, God created us for Himself (Colossians 1:16). He is not going to share us with any idols of this world, and those who have this world as their lover, are guilty of spiritual adultery because they are being unfaithful to their Creator, the one that deserves all our heart, our soul, and our mind (Matthew 22:37: Romans 12:2; 2 Corinthians 6:16-17; James 4:1-7).

Now, since we are the offspring of God, if our ways are His ways and our thoughts, His thoughts, we will have the same understanding of relationship as He does. We will not be Ok with sharing our spouse with anyone else, and we will love our spouse as our one and only. So technically, having more than one spouse is not about love at all. Rather it is all about lust. When a man loves a woman, he tends to favor her over all others. His love for her will also motivate him to be faithful to her and her alone, and therefore, he would not feel comfortable or even consider having sex with another woman.

So again, one man with many wives is not about love. If anything, it's about dominance and the women he is married to are no more than slaves to him. The word of God doesn't give a man any right to mistreat his wife, but if she is obligated to share him with other women, she is being mistreated by him, and he doesn't love her. Now, if any man foolishly gives the impression that he believes that a man should have the right to more than one wife, can the same man accept a woman having the right to more than one husband?

I guarantee you not a single man in all the earth would be OK with sharing the woman he loves with other men. However, if God allowed a man the right to do it, to avoid showing favoritism, he would also have to allow women the same right. God didn't create the world as a place for just. Marriage is not a man thing. It is for both men and women. One can't be married without the other. Just as the wife is to satisfy her husband only, the husband is to satisfy his wife only. However, he can't be faithful to her if he is married to her and a few more. Not only does the husband have authority over the wife's body, but the wife has authority over the husband's body also. A man can't neglect his wife's sexual needs and sex with other women is considered neglect! Therefore, any man or woman, who is married but having sex with someone other than their spouse is an adulterer, and they will be punished if they refuse to repent. This brings us back to the golden rule implemented by God to help us understand what it means to love. If we truly love a person, we will not do anything to them that we wouldn't want them to do unto us (Matthew 7:12). Another way to put this is, "treat others like you want to be treated."

Let the foolish man ask himself, "Would I be OK with my wife having a second husband and sex partner?" If your response to the question is no, obviously you know it's not right and that it doesn't even make sense for two women to have to share the same man when there are enough men and women in the world for every man to have his own and every woman to have her own. The marriage chaos exists because of man's rebellion against God.

Lastly, God is a merciful God and He will not punish those who are ignorant of the truth. Many women have been brainwashed and have no clue that they are being oppressed, and not receiving genuine love from the man that they acknowledge as their husband. They are being taken advantage of by men who do not perceive women to be created equal with the same rights as men. I'm convinced that many of the men who have multiple wives know the truth. The word of God teaches that our conscience reveals to us when we do things that are not right to do. Therefore, we cannot mistreat people and not that it's wrong. We can only decide to do it anyway. Chapter 10 will reveal who God created marriage for and why. .

CHAPTER 10
Marriage is for Believers

The word of God is a light unto the path of the righteous. It is the lamp unto our feet. It is what bread that we live by. Because we live by the word of God, we have a desire to do what pleases our Lord. Therefore, we long to be married to someone we can call our own and enjoy sexual pleasure with. We understand that God would have us not deprive our spouse of sex, and we do not have any intentions of ever cheating on our spouse. For this reason, we should only desire to be joined to someone who is spiritually compatible with us. If we go back to the beginning, we can clearly see that God has a relationship with Adam. We see God fellowshiping with Him and putting him over everything in the garden including the animals. Indeed, Adam has a relationship with God, which he could not have if he was walking in obedience to Him. Those who are in Christ are just as Adam was before he disobeyed God. We are in the light where God also is, and therefore, we have fellowship with Him. We can pray to Him and He'll hear our prayers and respond to us by His. We hear Him and proceed to do what He says unto.

It was God who felt that Adam should not be alone so He provided him with a mate. Not just any mate, but one who was spiritually compatible with him. If man obeys the Lord, he will only desire a woman who also obeys the Lord. For how is it possible for two people to walk together if they don't agree! Can a man of God say that his wife is a good thing if she doesn't meet God's approval! Therefore, marriage is not intended for everybody. This is because every man and/or every woman does not obey God. If they refuse to obey God it is a 100% chance that marriage would be dishonored by them in one way or another. Let's face it! It's not for unbelievers. Paul gives us some good advice to follow in 2 Corinthians 6. It is there that we find these words: "Be not unequally yoked together with unbelievers: for what fellowship hath righteousness with unrighteousness? and what communion hath light with darkness" (14-16). Based on what Paul rights, believers and unbelievers are like night and day. It is the difference between good and evil, right and wrong. When two people become a partnership, they have to agree with one another. They have to have the same mind and judgment. Well, do believers and unbelievers have the same desires? Do they think alike? The answer, no. Believers are traveling down the narrow and straight path that leads to eternal life. However, the unbeliever is traveling the wide and crowded way that leads to destruction. The righteous are children of the light and the unrighteous are children of darkness. The darkness cannot comprehend the light. Those who love darkness will come to the light where God is. Therefore, a believer and an unbeliever live two different lifestyles and they'll never agree on how marriage should be. Believers are spiritual minded and we walk according to the spiritual and fulfill not the lust of the flesh. The unbelievers, on the other hand, are carnal minded, hostile toward God, making it impossible for them to please God. As followers of Jesus Christ, we are lovers of God rather than lovers of pleasure. It's the other way around for the unbelievers. They're conformed to the world. They love the world. They love the things in the world. They have friendship with the world. They have a love for money and material things. They want to go and come and see all the splendor of the world. They walk in the counsel of the ungodly and desire to be where the sinners are. The children of God have no interest in what the children of darkness have an interest in. We have nothing in common with the unrighteous. There will be much conflict in the marriage. Jesus said that the world hates those who belong to him, but if we belong to the world, the world then loves us. So, how can a believer and an unbeliever enjoy one another when one loves God and the other loves the world! Unbelievers are selfish individuals who are only concerned about pleasing their flesh. They're not going to want to have a discussion about God from time to time. They're not going to have a desire to read the word of God or do ministry work. It will all be boring to them. Going to a marriage with an unbeliever is also risky. There is no guarantee that they will stay. Neither is there a guarantee that they'll remain faithful to you. Some of them will have no problem cheating with someone they think they have something in common with. Then, there is the issue of the children. Believers will train up their children in the way of the Lord, but it's a good chance that their efforts will be somewhat complicated if married to an unbeliever. Money will also be an issue. A believer will be content with what they need, but an unbeliever will have a desire to spend up the money on pleasure. Some unbelievers can also be verbally and/or physically abusive when they don't get what they want. The last thing a man of God wants to have to deal with is a quarreling, nagging, or contentious wife, who is unruly and refuses to respect him as her head. Likewise, a godly woman doesn't want to have to be submissive to an alcoholic or drug addict husband, a man who loves to gamble, one that is lazy, or filled with rage, is verbally or physically abusive, etc. Before a believer goes into a marriage he or she must not forget how long God intends for the marriage to last. It's not a temporary relationship. Neither is it to be entered into lightly. This is why choosing someone who is spiritually compatible with you going into it, is imperative. Once you say, "I do" in the presence of many witnesses. The marriage is official. From that point on, you'll have to deal with the ungodly ways of your unbelieving spouse until death do apart (Romans 7:2). Women, please understand that the only authority you have, is saying yes to the man that you're willing to live the rest of your life in submission to. If he doesn't know God and you know he isn't going into the marriage, don't expect him to change simply because you married him. No, that you don't have the right in Christ to mouth off at him or deprive him of sexual satisfaction because you don't like his ungodly ways. The only thing you have the right to do is exemplify what is righteous in his sight with the hope that he'll be won over (1 Peter 3:1-3). Believers, we do not have the power to change anyone! So, do not put your confidence in the flesh. The same word of God that brought about a change in us, has the power to bring about a change in anyone. However, it's completely up to them to hear and believe. Marriage is supposed to be filled with love and joy, not misery. So, do not take a chance on a person who doesn't know the Lord.

Well, what if you went into a marriage out of the will of God, but soon after you got married, you die to the flesh, took up your cross, and you're now following the Lord? You must remain with your unbelieving spouse. You must love them and endure all things. Either they will come to Christ at some point or they will remain as they are until the day. Just remember that no matter what you might be dealing with, God's grace is still sufficient. Know that you can and you will do all things through Christ who strengthens us. I know that the devil will put the thought of divorce in your mind when things get tough or seem too hard to bear. However, there is never a time that God is not with us. Furthermore, divorce isn't God's answer to you just because you hate having to deal with the ways of your unbelieving spouse. The Lord only gives us one acceptable reason for divorce which I shall discuss in the next chapter. Besides, children benefit from us remaining married to the unbelieving spouse. Remember love thinketh not of its own, Paul said, and Jesus also died for us because He loved us (1 Corinthians 13:5; Romans 5:8). Chapter 11 will discuss the three ways out of a marriage and Satan desire to bring about division in all marriages where there is at least one person who believes in Jesus Christ.

CHAPTER 11
Marriage: Easy to Get Into, but Not Easy to Get Out

Everyday we hear of people getting married. Some marriages consist of people who don't know God; some with two people who know God; and some consist of one believer and an unbeliever. I believe that no two people married expecting to someday be going their separate ways. Unfortunately, just as couples are getting married every day, married couples are also getting divorced everyday. Whether some live by the word of God or not, either way, anything that God disapproves of is sin. It is for this reason that God is calling all people to repentance. However, we've already established that the unrighteous dishonor God in marriage. It is nothing for the unrighteous to get married today and be divorced tomorrow. Some have even been married multiple times, which also means they have been divorced several times also. Hopefully, you can see why marriage isn't for the unbeliever. So, it is understandable that those who do not obey God don't keep the marriage vows. However, the children of God are led by the Spirit of God (Romans 8:14). The Holy Spirit is not the spirit of man, but He is the Spirit of God. He is that Spirit of truth who teaches us all things and brings all things back to our remembrance. Only influences us to do what pleases God. The word teaches us that marriage is honorable in the sight of God and the marriage bedroom is undefiled (Hebrews 13:4). It also teaches in the same verse that whoremongers and adulterers shall be judged. This tells that there is never a time that it's important for people to get married to avoid fornication and that it is also important that people not commit adultery. We know that fornication is sex before marriage so adultery is something people commit while married. God gives us the right to have sex married. However, the only person that he gives us the right to have sex with, is the one that we married. Therefore, once a person is married they are off the market. This shouldn't be a problem for a person who lives to please God. We're not greedy. Instead, we are content with having what we need. Some of us need a spouse, but there is never a time when we need someone on the side. That's the mindset of the unrighteous. However, we truly love the person we married. Our faithfulness toward one another is the will of God and He receives glory as a result of it. Well, the adversary, also known as the devil, has a problem with God being glorified. He has a problem with people remaining together until death do them apart, which is the will of God (Romans 7:2).

When a married person goes outside of the undefiled marriage bedroom that they share with their spouse into the bed of another is called adultery. This type of sexual sin is more serious in the sight of God than simply someone not married having sex with another person not married. Fornicators are not required to be faithful, but what is the purpose of people getting married if they are only going to have sex with someone they're not married to anyway. Marriage is a solution to a problem! Love and faithfulness is a part of it. Unfortunately, many have neither love nor faithfulness entering a marriage. Because meant for two people to remain together, and enjoy sex with one another, He strongly dislikes adultery.

All through the word of God there is information concerning adultery. We know that Adam and his wife Eve were together until one of them died. Also, adultery is one of those obvious sins that no one needs to be made aware of. It is a sin that all who commit it want to keep it a secret. As I've said before, if you don't want anyone to know, you already know it's not right to do. King David comes to mind while discussing the topic of adultery. David did what Jesus taught that we shouldn't do. Jesus taught that if a man looks at a woman and lust for her in his heart, he is guilty of adultery (Matthew 5:28). Although we live to please God, we must give any place to the devil. Men, we have to spiritual pluck out our eyes daily, to prevent from being drawn away unto temptation. Believers, we must ensure that our spouses are receiving sexual satisfaction due to them. Depriving one another of sex, give place to Satan to tempt us.

Based on what Jesus said in verse 28 of Matthew, chapter 5, the act of adultery first starts in the heart. In Matthew, chapter 15, Jesus tells us that adultery comes forth from the heart (v. 19). Well, David's adulterous affair began with him looking upon Bathsheba while she was bathing. He invited her to the palace; he probably wined and dined her. He eventually fulfilled the lust of the heart by having sex with her, knowing she was another man's wife. Unfortunately, Bathsheba became pregnant and David wanted to cover up that he had been with her. This tells us that David knew that sleeping with Bathsheba was wrong. However, his attempt was to no avail because he could not get her husband to sleep with her. The only other option David had was to have Bathsheba's husband killed. David went from an adulterer to a murderer. Although David successfully hid his actions from people, God saw it all. David suffered consequences for his actions. The baby he had with Bathsheba became sick and died, David's wives were given to others. The sword never left his house, and David eventually ended up on a sick bed (2 Samuel 12:9-12. Ultimately, we reap what we sow. Also remember that adultery is also a sexual sin which is committed against the person's own body. Absolutely no one who commits adultery escapes consequences for their actions.

In the book of Leviticus laws, adulterers, both people who participated were to be put to death (20:10). Then, we have the woman Jezebel in Revelation, Chapter 2, who was given the opportunity to repent of her adultery, but did not. As a consequence of her action, God threw her on a sick bed and killed her children (20-22). Also, the men who were involved with her suffered tribulation.

According to what is written in Exodus 20, God said out of His own mouth, "Thou shall not commit adultery" (v. 14). Hebrews

13:4 also reveals to us that adulterers shall be punished. Lastly, Paul also tells us adulterers shall not inherit the kingdom of God (1 Corinthians 6:9; Galatians 5:19). The good thing is, God is merciful and He grants adulterers the opportunity to repent. Although David suffered consequences, he repented of his actions (2 Samuel 12:13). It is also important to know that repentance is not saying with your mouth, "Lord forgive me. It is what Jesus told the woman accused of adultery: "Go away and sin no more" (John 8:11). We do not read where David ever committed adultery again. His repentance was sincere. All sexual sins are dangerous. It is understanding for those who commit adultery to suffer from their actions. However, we can be sure that God doesn't want the innocent spouse to suffer right alone with their unfaithful spouse.

Many false teachers tell those who follow them that under no circumstance can a believer divorce their spouse. Because there are many false teachers in the world today, we must try every spirit to see if they are of God. If what they say contradicts what Jesus spoke, it is a lie. Jesus tells us in Matthew, chapter 19 and verse 9 that if a man divorces his wife for any reason other than fornication and the same man goes and marries another woman he is guilty of adultery. What Jesus taught is a difficult thing for a person who walks after the flesh. A person who doesn't know God doesn't want to wait until their spouse commits adultery to divorce them. They want to be able to divorce them for any reason they choose to. This would mean that if a man's wife nagged him, contented with him, or quarreled with him, he could use it as a justification for the divorce. Solomon spoke about these types of women in the book of Proverbs, but he doesn't instruct a man to divorce because of it. Instead, all he said was "it is better for a man to live in the wilderness than to live in the house with them" (Proverbs 21:19). This is why I said in the last chapter that believers should not marry unbelievers. The word of God doesn't permit believers to divorce their spouse just because we are irritated by them, or because they cuss a lot, drink alone, nag a lot and so on. Neither does it matter to God if we are married to an unbeliever. We still can't divorce them. There are only three reasons divorce can take place. Of course, the first is brought about by death (Romans 7:2). The second one way is, if our spouse commits adultery, which is highly unlike if they are walking in the Spirit. If it happens, it would more than likely be committed by an unbelieving spouse. The third and final reason is, if our unbelieving spouse decides that they no longer want to be married to us, Paul said, let them go (1 Corinthians 7:15). Based on what Paul says, marriage was never meant to be experienced by unbelievers because they will not follow God's instructions for marriage. Besides, we do not have the power to make anyone remain in marriage. If they want out the marriage they are obviously not a follower of the Lord. Especially if adultery did not occur. Believers do not allow Satan to deceive you into following your gut feeling. We don't do what seems right to us. We are led by the Spirit of God to obey the word of God. Chapter 12 will discuss the other things that are important for a good marriage.

CHAPTER 12
Marriage Consist of More Than Just Sex

There is much much more involved in marriage than sex. Just as we all come into the world as infants, we also began our spiritual rebirth as infants in the faith. To grow unto a level of spiritual maturity we must receive nourishment from the same word of God that caused us to become born of God. If we have truly tasted that the Lord is gracious after hearing the word of God, we will develop a craven for the word of God as a newborn baby craves its mother's milk and grow by it (1 Peter 2:2-3).

In the faith we crawl before we walk, we go from unskilled to skilled (Hebrews 5:13-14). At some point, we will be equipped to discern what is good and what is evil. We can be confident that seeking God diligently will result in us being greatly rewarded with necessary wisdom, knowledge, and understanding (Hebrews 11:6; Proverbs 1:7; 2:6). Having knowledge, wisdom, and understanding helps us to become mature and equip us for marriage. Truth is, sex doesn't require much work nor does it require commitment from those who engage in it. . Marriage, on the hand, cannot go the distance that God purpose it to on just sex alone. For this reason, not everybody has what it takes to be married. One thing is for sure, it is foolish to go into marriage without proper understanding first. The fool says, "Let's get married" without absolutely no understanding. However, "get understanding" is what the word of God tells us to do (Proverbs 4:7).

God would have us attempt to figure marriage out as we go along. Marriage is honorable in sight, but we fail to use the marriage manual, that which is good could easily dishonor God. Do not follow the advice of the ungodly who say, "just do it. Learn from your experience." Many people have ruined their lives using experience as the best teacher. Experience can lead to patience, but some things are better done having knowledge before experiencing it. Therefore, since marriage is founded by God, that makes Him only one qualified to direct toward marriage, in it, and through it. Can we figure out on our own how to worship God! Are we not required to live by His spoken word (Matthew 4:4)? So apart from the word of God, we cannot know what is required of us. We must learn from God our roles and responsibilities. We're born with the ability to be a husband or wife. We become such and if we're going to wear title, we must be able to perform our duties.

Maturity is one of the things deemed necessary for marriage. Where there is no maturity, there can be no love. The two go hand and hand. Marital love is not some warm and fuzzy feeling. It's not founded on happy times and good memories. Instead, it is built on unconditional love. In fact, the word of God commands a man to love his wife with the same love that he demonstrates toward his own body (Ephesians 5:28). She deserves to be nourished and cherished as if she is a part of him. His love for her must also be unconditional love which is compared to the love that Christ has for the church. Christ loved us so much that He died for us (v. 25; Romans 5:8). This something we need to know going into marriage and not after. We love each other so much that our love does what Paul said love does: "beareth all things, believeth all things, hopeth all things, and endureth all things" (1 Corinthians 13:7). It will take love and maturity for a wife to submit herself unto her husband (Ephesians 5:24; Colossians 3:18). Many women get offended when they are told that a wife must submit herself unto her husband. They often interpret the word submission as a word that implies that she must be her husband's slave, but that is not at all what it implies. It is difficult for a man to lead his wife if she nags, quarrels, if she is unruly. According to what is written in the book of Proverbs, a man is better off living alone than to live with a woman that refuses to submit to him (Proverbs 7:11; 9:13; 11:22; 21:9). A godly woman married to a godly man will have no problem being satisfied with the love she receives from him. Her submission to him will not be perceived as mistreatment (1 Peter 3:7). Love is respectful, and therefore, because they both love each other, they should have no problem fulfilling their role in the marriage. Although the husband is the head of the wife, he has an obligation to love her. He can't verbally or physically abuse her and continue having a relationship with God. His mistreatment will hinder his prayer and no man of God wants that (1 Peter 7).

I think about what Paul said, in one of his letters to the Corinthians. He said, "when I was a child I spoke as a child, I understood as a child, I thought as a child, but when I became a man, I put away childish things" (1 Corinthians 13:11, KJV). When two people get married they should have already put away childish things. What we cannot do in marriage is behave selfishly. especially when it comes to having sex. I say this because, many spouses are sexually deprived by their spouse, and purposely. Perhaps it is the main reason for so much infidelity in a lot of marriages. However, believers have an obligation to be mature and loving. Even if disagreements arise in our marriage, we must not deprive one another of sex. We are to do unto others as we would have others do unto us. Besides, it is sin for us to withhold sex (1 Corinthians 7:4). An immature person will not care about what is right. They will selfishly do what they want to do which will negatively affect the marriage. This is exactly why maturity is necessary. Perhaps, create a man and a woman and not a girl and a boy in the beginning. Some things are only meant to be done at an adult age, and marriage is one of them.

Companionship is also a part of marriage. From the beginning, God determined that a man needed companionship, who could also be a helper to him (Genesis 2:18). Paul instructed the older woman to teach the younger women how to care for the children and love her husband (Titus 2:3-5). The man will provide for her and she will manage the home while he works. Also, they will enjoy fellowship with one another, eat together, praise God together, study the word of God together, do ministry work together, wake up to each other and lie down together, parent children together, etc. There is nothing like having someone to call your own, who can be of your bone and of your flesh, to be one with you until death do you apart (Genesis 2:23). Lastly, the only one closer to a man than his wife is God our Savior and Lord. What a beautiful thing to have someone to share the rest of your life with. Chapter 13 will show how living with someone for years is not the same as being married for years.

CHAPTER 13
Living and Sleeping Together Doesn't Make It a Marriage

It is a wonderful thing for two people to remain in a long-term relationship for a lifetime. In fact, God wants a man to have companionship until the duration of his life. However, there are many people who have been living together as a couple for years, who think that their long-term relationship qualifies them as husband and wife. However, God would not have us to navigate through life doing what seems right in our eyes (Proverbs 14:12). He didn't create us to lean on our own understanding (Proverbs 3:5). Anyone who believes that he or she can direct their own path and not seek God, proves to hate knowledge and despise wisdom and understanding (Proverb 1:7, 22). Marriage did not originate with us; we are not its founder. Neither does it exist without definition and instruction. Indeed, marriage consists of one man and a woman, but no marriage can be a secret and honor God. Those who are truly married want others to know it. We also want it certified. We want to be recognized as Mr and Mrs so on and son in public. We cannot be ashamed of anything we do unto the glory of God. In fact, we are literally told that whatsoever we do, we are to do it as representative of Jesus Christ (Colossians 3:17). Jesus also told us that if we are ashamed of Him, He would be ashamed of us, and if we fail to acknowledge before men, He will not acknowledge us when He returns (Luke 9:26; Matthew 10:32-33). Keeping our relationship with someone a secret from everyone is obviously, sin. We can't keep our relationship with Jesus a secret and represent Him at the same time! Therefore, if marriage is honorable in the sight of God, how can it honor Him if it is kept a secret! Furthermore, We are obligated to let our light shine before other people (Matthew 5:16). People see us representing God in our relationship. They need to be able to see our change from promiscuity to happily married. No matter how long two people have been in a relationship and living with one another, it is not the same as being officially married. A man might say, "technically, we marry because we've been together for many years as a couple." However, a man can be sexually involved with one woman for years is still not anything other than a fornicator. The only difference is, they just don't live together. Jesus doesn't see it the way a sinful man sees it. He established in the beginning that a man leaves his parents and cleaves to a wife (Genesis 2:24). This is bigger than him having sex with. He could have stayed with his parents and did that. Jesus gives us a good picture of what is fornication and adultery. In a conversation Jesus had with a Samaritan woman, He tells her to go get her husband (John 4:16). Surely, He knew whether the woman had a husband or not. The woman's response was, I don't have a husband (v. 17). It is true that she didn't have a legal husband. By law, she was anyone's wife. Jesus didn't disagree with her. He told her that she was right, that she doesn't have a husband in the same verse. However, He reveals something to us in what He tells the woman next. He said to her that she's had five husbands and the man she is currently involved with is not her husband (v. 18). OK, can a person have more than one spouse? The answer is, no. However, a person can be guilty of having sex with several people. A person can also be sexually involved with someone who is lawfully married to someone else. The Samaritan was guilty of fornication which spiritually joins people together, and she was guilty of adultery which spiritually unjoins two people who God had joined together. So, this tells us that unless two people are lawfully married, although they might be spiritually joined together, it is not because God joined them, but because of fornication.

This is where the governing authorities come into play. We are told that there is no government but God who ordained government (Romans 13:1). It is the government's job to maintain order, anything that law requires, we are obligated by God to obey if what we are asked to do doesn't go against His written word. Therefore, we are told that all who resist government law, are not just resisting government, but God also. All governments require marriage certification. Also, all governments have established laws in place for adultery. If two people are living together as husband and wife uncertified, they're not officially married, nor can either of them be guilty of adultery. However, they are guilty of fornication. This takes us to Hebrew 13:4. The only bedroom that is undefiled, the one that a man shares with his lawful wife. The verse concludes by saying, "But whoremongers and adulterers God shall judge."

Shacking up is not influenced by the God of heaven and earth. Be not deceived. Everything that exists, has an identification. Without proof, there would be no accountability. Being required to have a marriage license or certificate is no different than being required to have a driver's license as proof that we're legal to drive. If a person is pulled over and doesn't have a valid license, they are guilty of breaking the law. God made all things with an identity. A man is identified as a male. A woman is identified as a female (Genesis 1:27). All the animals, fish, birds, and every creeping thing has an identity. Every mountain and every body of water, and everything else that exists, has an identity. We can't call a man a woman or a woman a man and not be guilty of lying. If we're born a male, we can't rightfully be a female. Neither can a female rightly be a male. It is our God given identity. Likewise, saying that you are married without proof of your marriage makes you a liar, and God hates a lying tongue (Proverb 6:17; Revelation 21:1). Jesus said that those who hear and believe shall be set free by the truth(John 8:31-32). I hope that reaches the hearts of many who are living in fornication thinking they are common law married. If you truly love the person you're living with, make it official. Marry them. In Chapter 13, we will deal with how what we see with our eyes, hear with our ears, and entertain in our mind can lead to sexual immorality.

CHAPTER 14
Hear No Evil, See No Evil, Think No Evil, and Speak No Evil

The word of God says, "If your eye causes you to sin, you should pluck it out." It also reveals that a man can commit the sin of lust by looking at a woman with lust in his heart for her (Matthew 5:28-29, KJV). This tells me that it is necessary for us to have disciplined eyes, that it's not good to stare at a person's body. We can best believe that from the beginning of man's existence, what God hates is often appealing to the eyes (Genesis 3:6). Seduction is a real thing. It is a powerful weapon of the enemy which is used to tempt people into sexually immoral thoughts and actions. We can and we will desire what we see with our eyes if we entertain it and there are plenty of verses written for our warning. It is especially important for men, who are visual creatures, to guard our eyes. Women can be very appealing to our eyes, and it would be hard to stare at them and not lust after them. David has already proved to us what could happen when a man stares at the beauty of a woman. David's son Solomon tells us in the book of Proverb something that the wise will take heed to. He is giving advice on how to keep oneself away from the evil woman (Proverbs 6:24). His advice to us is, "Lust not after her beauty in thine heart; neither let her take thee with her eyelids" (v. 6). Because of sin these bodies of flesh have a desire to be satisfied and we are not strong enough to look and not lust. Therefore, to avoid lusting with our eyes, we must stare not. Satan understands that sin has an affect on the eyes. Not only did he persuade Eve to lust with her eyes in Genesis 3, he also tried to persuade Jesus in a like manner. According to what is written, the devil took Jesus up to a high mountain where he could see all the world kingdoms and the things in them (Matthew 4:8). After showing Him the pleasures of the world, he promised to give Jesus access to such things, if Jesus would agree to worship him (v. 9). Of course, Jesus did not worship the devil. Instead, He became the example for us to follow. He resisted him (v. 10-11). We too, must do what is written in the word of God by having the word in our heart.

From the beginning, God made clothing necessary so that the naked body would not be exposed publicly because of sin (Genesis 3:21). Everything God does serves a purpose. If lust is possible by staring at a woman with clothes on, surely, it is a difficult thing for a man to avoid lusting after a woman who has no clothes on. This takes me back to David. According to what is written, David was on his roof when he saw Bathsheba washing herself and noticed how beautiful she was (2 Samuel 11:2). Surely, Bathseba did not have any clothes on, and she was beautiful on top of that. It would be hard for any man to look at a woman undressed and not lust for her. He looked and with his eyes, he lusted, which led him to pursue her and eventually They engaged in sexual intercourse with one another (v. 4). Sex with her resulted in pregnancy (v. 5). David was drawn away by his own lust and enticed which can happen to anyone, who gives place to the devil (James 1:14).

May we learn from David what not to do that we might avoid finding ourselves in a similar predicament. Unfortunately, there are many who have eyes full of sexual lust. All around us there is "peeping Tom." These are individuals who are addicted to looking at the nakedness of others. They are known for peeking into people's windows, installing cameras in people's homes, recording people, or taking pictures of them with their cell phone without them knowing, and so on. They do not just look unto lust, but the lust is then manifested into sexual immoral acts such as masturbation, rape, sexual assault, and the like. Lusting with the eyes simply comes for the sexual immoral act.

Many men are just like the "peeping Tom." They just haven't been labeled as such. I am willing to admit that before I came to

Christ, I was guilty of staring at women without them knowing, fantasizing about them, and even satisfying myself afterwards. I was also addicted to porn..

From my own experience, I can bear witness that it is necessary to spiritually pluck out the eyes, like Jesus said (Matthew 5:29). We must be wise to give no place to the devil by understanding how powerful the lust of sin is. The flesh is weak, and therefore, it must be our heart's desire to do what pleases God. It took the power of God to put to death lust in my life. By receiving the word of God in my heart and by the word of God remaining in me, my desire to see what I used to entertain myself with, is no longer my desire, but the desire of my heart now is to do what pleases the Lord (1 John 3:9).

Let me also add that being married and the fact that the marriage bedroom is undefiled, is not to be misinterpreted as "it's OK for a man and his wife to look at porn, during, or after sex. A man should not be lusting after women and a woman should not be lusting after other men under any circumstances. It is sin! For those of us who are married, it is adultery. It is impossible for a person to truly love their spouse if they have eyes full of lust. God has given a man to his wife and a wife to her husband. We have one another to look at and desire. We should not need to see the nakedness of others or others having sex, to get us in the mood for one another. Our relationship is founded on love. Longing for one another intimately isn't difficult for two people who truly love each other. Only those who walk after the flesh need something to see or hear to get them in the mood to have sex with someone.

Clothing can also play a role in enticing people. The word of God gives us a detailed description of the attire of an adulterous/immoral woman. It says that such a woman wears the attire of a harlot or a prostitute if you prefer (Proverbs 7:10). This lets me know that there is a certain dress code designed to make a woman sexually appealing to the eyes, and if she desires to be sexually appealing, she obviously wants men to lust after her body and/or beauty. If she is seeking attention with the intentions of seducing men, her ways prove to be immoral although some that we see publicly are simply ignorant to the truth. Either way, it is important for men not to look and also important for women to be taught that clothes that are revealing are inappropriate.

The women of God cannot be ignorant of what is an appropriate dress code (2 Timothy 2:9; 1 Peter 3:1-5). They know the importance of not causing men to stumble. Furthermore, a married woman is off limits to any other man so why would she dress publicly like she doesn't belong to anyone! Such would also be disrespectful to her husband, who married her to have her to himself. He is the only person entitled to see her nakedness. If other men are privileged to see what he sees, he is not married to a godly woman, but a harlot. The same goes for the men. Wives do not want their husbands lusting after other women or other women lusting after their husband.

The fact that many desire to look upon the nakedness of others is the reason why we have places of adult entertainment. Sexual lust is big business. Because it is such, there exist exotic dance clubs, penthouse and playboy, pornography, phone sex businesses, and the list goes on. The word of God teaches that a person is blessed who doesn't go in the way of sinners (Psalms 1:1). Therefore, we must make every effort to guard our eyes.

Just like our eyes, we must also be very careful about entertaining certain conversations, listening to the words of explicit and obscene lyrics and/or reading materials to avoid sexual lust. People who are sexually immoral specialize in flattery. Yes, people are seduced all the time with sweet sounding words or by lips dripping with honey as the book of Proverbs puts it (Proverbs 5:3). Solomon tells us to keep away from the flattery of the tongue of a strange woman (6:24). There is also a connection between flattery and lying. The father of those who act in movies and perform songs for the love of money is the devil, and the work of their father is what they do (John 8:44). In fact, every sinful person those who love darkness rather than the light are of the devil (1 John 3:8). "Like father, like son," so to speak! There is no truth found in flattery. Flattery is of the devil, it's all lies. When you're listening to songs, oftentimes you're only listening to good sounding lies. Be not deceived! It's not just harmless entertainment." Listening to sexually explicit and obscene words and/or lyrics accompanied by music makes its way into the heart and mind unto lustful desire. Eventually, the sin that enters into the heart will come forth from the heart in the form of sexual words, thoughts, and actions (Matthew 15:18-19). I've heard many songs in my lifetime that glorified adultery and fornication.

For years, like many still do today, I would listen to a song and be in the mood for the sex described in the song and even wanted to so-called, "make love" to the same sexual immoral songs. It's nothing for the lyrics of songs to get stuck in your head to the point where you find yourself singing the lyrics frequently along with the music or without it. Not only that, but we're also all probably guilty of thinking that those songs filled with sexual immorality were good at the time. We called such songs good in our ignorance, but once we came into relationship with Jesus Christ our Lord, we now know that such songs were planted by Satan and ought not be listened to. Under no circumstances should such songs end up in the marriage bedroom. If music is your "cup of tea" be mindful of the music you entertain yourself with. Sex with our spouse is a reality, not a fantasy and certain music will indeed cause the mind to go beyond reality into vain imagination.

This brings us to the various reading materials that Satan plants to lead many people into a life of sexual immorality. I have encountered people whose sexual adventures were the result of some of the books they read. Not many years ago, there was a book called, "Fifty Shades of Gray," which I'm certain contributed to a lot of risky sexual adventures, fornication, and infidelity. All sinful entertainment is influenced by Satan. As the god of this world, he is in control of the entertainment industry. He gives people platforms every day in exchange for the splendors of the world (Matthew 4:9; John 8:44). Indeed, he is succeeding at blinding the mind of many, who have heard the gospel of Jesus Christ. The riches that they receive from Satan is just too good to turn so for the money and material things, many choose to take pleasure in unrighteousness. Yes, the love of money is the main influence of the evil things that people do (1 Timothy 6:10).

It is imperative that we guard our eyes and ears, but it is also important that we are mindful of what we put our mind on. Let us not assume that what we think doesn't matter to God. We are not exempt from having sexual immoral thoughts. It is our responsibility to walk in the Spirit to avoid fulfilling the lust of the flesh (Romans 6:12-13; Galatians 5:16). Adultery can and will be committed in a person's mind if a person does not guard their eyes, and ears. Just like what we look at with our eyes, what we hear also becomes what we think on. I can't count the number of times I entertained sexually immoral thoughts, or shall I say, "dirty thoughts," and even now, such thoughts pop in my mind from time to time, with the hope that I would entertain them. People you haven't had sex with in years, visions of you and them can pop up in your mind. Satan wants us to reminisce or to perceive our past as the so-called, "Good old days." However, we must cast out such thoughts because what the unrighteous perceive as the "Good old days," were not good days but evil days. We were separated from God at the time. We are new creatures now and we're not to look back, but to press forward toward our goal of inheriting the kingdom of God.

We are also judged for the thoughts we entertain, because there are many people who are not able to do sexually immoral acts, due to disabilities or old age, but they still can have sexually immoral thoughts. This reminds me of what Jesus said about what comes forth from a sinful heart. He tells us that evil thoughts come forth from the heart, which means that we can think sexually immoral thoughts, we can commit adultery and fornication in our heart (Matthew 15:18-19). Paul tells us what thoughts are good thoughts. He says, "Whatsoever things are true, honest, pure, lovely, of good report" (Philippians 4:8). We might not be able to see what people think but the God who made us has access to the hidden secrets of the heart and to all the paths of men (Psalms 139:2-23; Proverbs 5:21; Hebrews 4:12). Furthermore, entertaining evil thoughts is no different than committing evil acts. Now, it is not sin for a man to entertain thoughts of the intimate times he shares with his wife. A man and his wife should have thoughts about each other. They are lovers and many couples have been such for a long, long, long time. We can be certain that God has no problem with a man making love to his wife or a woman making love to her husband in her mind.

Lastly, God must have control of our tongue also. Absolutely no corrupt communication should proceed out of our mouth (Ephesians 4:29). We can't use filthy language, vulgarity during sex (Colossians 3:8). So, let us who are married be wise; let us guard our eyes, ears, mouth, and thoughts. Let us be the living sacrifice that God accepts as holy in His sight (Romans 12:1). In chapter 14, will focus on all the lies that people believe about sex unto their own ruin.

CHAPTER 15
Believing the Lies About Sex

Some tend to think that they are wiser than God and can avoid the consequences of sexual sin. The truth is, if they can avoid them, God is a liar and doesn't exist. I make this bold statement because it is impossible for God to lie or his word to return unto Him void (Numbers 23:19; Isaiah 55:11). The condom that God has given unto mankind is marriage. It is the only undefiled way to have sex (Hebrews 13:4). According to Galatians 6:8, if a person sow to the flesh, they shall also reap of corruption. Corruption and destruction go hand and hand. What is being said in the verse is no different from what Paul speaks in other places. We know by 1 Corinthians 6:19, that fornicators and adulterers eventually suffer in their body. We know by what is written in Romans 1:27 that gay men suffer a due penalty in themselves. The book of Numbers speaks of a plaque that killed 24,000 men because of sexual immorality (25:9). Verse 1 proves that it happened as a result of whoredom. We can be certain that the plague was nothing more than a sexually transmitted disease. Just as sexually transmitted spreaded way back then, they are still spreading now, and many are dying because of it. If God said that the sexual immoral shall be judged, they will be judged. Evil men have invented evil ways to make people feel comfortable disobeying God. They do the work of their father the devil. Satan wants to see people's lives ruined, but he also wants them to think that evil is good. People like the feeling of sex, but they don't like the consequences for their sin. Therefore, Satan provides them evil remedies: condoms, birth control, night after pill, antibiotics for diseases, and the like. This reminds me of the sorcerers and wise men that Pharoah used to compete with the power of God. The staff of Moses turn into a snake. Then, the magicians produced serpents also using enchantment. After they were done, the Serpent that the power of God brought about, swallowed up the magician's serpents

(Exodus 7:10-13). What this tells me is, man can't invent anything that is "GOD PROOF." In fact, God did many other things by the hands of Moses that the Magicians could not duplicate or cause to go away (8:17-19). This also tells me that sorcerers (scientists) of today might be able to produce things to suppress the consequences of sexual immorality, but they could never cure anything that is God sent. Besides, Satan's kingdom is divided against the kingdom of God (Matthew 12:24-28). He does not have a desire to heal the sickness of anyone, or to keep anyone alive, for he cometh but to kill, steal, and destroy (John 10:10). Satan is a liar and a murder, too (John 8:44). Be not deceived! Satan is exalted by deceiving people into sicknesses and diseases. It was him who caused boils to appear on the body of Job (Job 2:4-7). Since Satan doesn't have any love for mankind, we can be sure that even the medicines that the children of the devil invent for sexually transmitted diseases, are intended to work against the body whether the inventors know it or not.

God has one rule for sex, "NO SEX UNTIL YOU'RE MARRIED!" The wise will humble themselves to the voice of God and let Him be true and every man a liar in their heart. Those who encourage you to have safe sex or tell you that you can protect yourself from the consequences are liars. It is the lying spirits that say things like, "It's natural for people to have sex with everyone that they're sexually attracted to," or "Have sex responsibly." Just like Eve, people are allowing Satan to deceive them into accepting evil as good. "Woe to them who call evil good and good evil" (Isaiah 5:20). He has convinced some that there is no harm in using such evil inventions to facilitate safe sex and to prevent pregnancy. The problem with this is sex is not as simple as a man going into a woman. Besides, a woman can't get pregnant if she obeys the will of God. People can't contract sexually transmitted diseases if they're not having sex. If it was good to have sex with people we're not married to, no protection would be needed.

Normally, there are things done to accomplish sexual arousal, which contributes to the production of vaginal fluid, semen, and the erection of the penis. This is where the problem comes into the picture. When people are infected with disease, the infection doesn't simply remain inside the vaginal area or on the penis. The infection can be anywhere in the genital areas, inside the mouth, about the lips, in the anal area, and so on. It is difficult to avoid contact diseases during sexual intercourse. Kissing and oral sex, which is often a part of sex, can and does lead to the transmission of sexually transmitted diseases. It's nothing for people who think that they are being safe to become careless. I am 100% certain that if a person is promiscuous, at some point, they're going to end up with some unwanted infection.

If there are no consequences ever suffered for disobedience, people wouldn't see the importance of turning from sin (Romans 1:27 Corinthians 6:18). God loves us! Therefore, He must discipline us to get us in line or to keep us in line (Hebrews 12:6). What the devil means for bad, God uses it for the good. He uses the things that people suffer to get their attention, to deter them from what the devil is using to destroy human life.

All God wants us to do is stop doing what He hates. If you keep sleeping around, you'll keep having issues with your body. If you keep seeking the same treatments over and over again, eventually the treatments that only suppress the condition will stop suppressing. The more people use them, the more you destroy your immune system. If it becomes weak enough, it will not be able to fight against the invaders of the body. One way or another God will get the attention of the disobedient. They will either stop or the suffering will get worse and eventually destroy them, if not lead to their death. Be not deceived! You don't have it all under control as you think. It is also impossible to determine whether a person is infected by simply looking at them. Some people appear to be clean and fresh but many of them are carriers of infectious diseases (Proverbs 7:17-

18). The last thing you want is to fall for the beautiful, sweet-smelling flesh of a diseased person unto a life changing experience (Proverbs 6:25-28). Many are fooled daily by stylish hair, decorative clothing, makeup, perfumes, and colognes that gives the illusion that the person is safe to have sex with. Some will achieve sexual satisfaction even if it means giving others what they're carrying. Will you accept the truth that sex outside of marriage is never safe. Where do you think the unwanted bumps, blisters, rashes, odors, and discharges come from!. Do you really trust the people you're having sex with! Do you also trust science, too! If so, that is the first mistake you made. Only God cannot lie. We must trust God, not man. Ladies, a man might start with a condom but when the act is over, you'll find that he no longer has it on. This is what many do; they take it off right in the middle of sex. Sometimes people are so caught up that things go unnoticed. However, this is the risk that is taken having sex outside of marriage. It is also true that most sexually immoral women don't request that a condom be used by their partner. They, too, don't like the way condoms feel inside of them. Neither do they want to be irritated after the use of one.

It is up to each person to make a conscious decision whether they will obey the truth when they hear it or fall for the lie and be deceived. Falling for the big butt, the wide hips, the big breasts, the juicy lips, and the many other physical features that are used to lure people into a trap that leads to many hurtful lust unto the destruction of many. Word of advice, "Flee the very presence of evil, run from fornication (1 Corinthians 6:18)! Care about your body; it is the temple of God (v. 19). Lastly, it is important for us to debunk the myths about sex that also lead to the destruction of many people. God said, "My people perish for lack of knowledge" (Hosea 4:6). However, if you read the rest of the verse you come to realize that the only way people can perish is by rejecting the knowledge. Many will turn a deaf ear to what I say and continue in the direction of destruction.

Those lack of understanding result in people basing sex on outward beauty, the size and shape of certain parts of a person's body. A certain anatomy type or physique has nothing to do with good sex. It's all good sex or God would have spoken otherwise. Furthermore, if it wasn't good, people would continue to chase its pleasurable feeling. The truth is, there is only the bad way, which is, with someone you're not married to and the good way, in the marriage bedroom. Any penis will work with any vagina, and the saying, "bigger is better" is a devil's lie. If you believe the lie, you take the risk of destroying yourself. A desire for more than what you have is not influenced by God! God has no desire for you to perish.

Sadly, people are undergoing surgeries, taking hormone pills, using pumps for the sake of having better sex because they fell for the devil's lie. In the process, many have destroyed themselves by altering their penis size, even the women who have had surgery to shrink the size of their vagina and to enlarge their breasts and buttocks. If it can't be accomplished naturally without the aid of science, there is nothing good about it. If it isn't good, it's not the will of God, either. There are consequences when mixing artificial and natural together and/or taking manmade enhancement drugs for the sake of sexual performance. Many men have died from heart attacks due to the use of sexual enhancement drugs. Nothing can or will work like the original creation of God. Neither can man better the creation of God in any way! God made sexual pleasure easy to obtain, and we don't have to make any changes to what we have already.. If we are content with what we have and trust in God, we shall have absolutely no problem achieving sexual pleasure at the right time. There is no embarrassing one another or belittling one another in a marriage where the couple is godly, loving, and mature. When a person finally comes to realize that there is no special remedy for good sex, they have officially been set free. Chapter 15 will reveal something worse than a person secretly being unfaithful to their spouse.

CHAPTER 16
The Married Sexually Immoral Couple

I'm sure by the chapter title that some will say, "how can a married couple be sexually immoral. Cheating is running rampant in the world today. Normally, the unfaithful spouse does everything to keep their infidelity secret. Although the cheater doesn't want to be found out about, the reason for keeping it a secret is not because they are ashamed of what they're doing. They don't feel sorry for what they're doing. Cheaters do not want to get caught because they don't want to lose the comfort and the stability provided for them. Then, there is the issue of alimony, court expenses, child support, etc. There is a lot to lose behind adultery. So, unless the cheater gets caught they always return to the comfort of their home and sleep beside their spouse after they've been on a sexual adventure with their lover. In words, cheaters want their cake and eat it, so to speak. Their unloving selfish individuals, who are nothing but "lovers of themselves. They are cold-hearted and compulsive liars; their father is the devil.

Eventually, God exposes the adulterer. In fact, in a marriage where at least one spouse is one of His, adultery is short-lived. We know this because God protects His own. He's not going to put more on us than we can bear. Furthermore, when a person is obedient to the Lord, all of their experiences that are of no fault of our own, is allowed to make us a better servant for Him. All things work for the good of those who love the Lord" (Roman 8:28). We are given a picture of this! God allowed Satan to do certain things to Job that He might prove Job's unwavering faith in Him (Job 1:7-22; 2:1-10).

So, it is established that adultery is normally done in secret and is normally committed by one spouse although there are instances where both spouses are secretly cheating on one another. Now the question to ask is, can there be anything in a marriage than being cheated on? What's worse than one person in the marriage committing adultery or both the husband and the wife secretly cheating on one another, is both the husband and the wife committing adultery together as a couple. In other words, they consent to engaging in sexual intercourse with other couples. This type of sexual immorality is called swinging, but what it should be is called wicked foolery! Marriage is supposed to honor God and if two people would dare consent to adultery, their marriage is an absolute waste of time. The truth is, they should have remained unmarried because their marriage isn't a solution to anything. Can you see how wicked and disgusting and meaningless such a marriage is. Such a couple is obviously unrighteous. No one who truly loves the Lord would ever consent to their spouse having sex with someone other than them.

Can you imagine the sicknesses and diseases that are contracted and/or spread by those who swing. Perhaps, these individuals assume that such a sexual encounter is safer because it is experienced with other married couples. However, if a married couple will consent to having sex with another married couple, who's to say that they haven't already had sex with other married couples, who has also been having sex with other married couples. Only a fool would think that just because two people are married, they are without infections. Besides, those who do such a thing are obviously out of the will of God and can't be trusted. Just like any person living a sexually immoral life, it is a good chance that they're not honest with those they sleep with, and eventually, fornicators suffer a due penalty within themselves (Romans 1:27; 1 Corinthians 6:18).

We can also be certain that the marriage of those who swing soon end in the divorce. What do you expect to happen if a man allows his wife to have sex with another man and if a woman consents to her husband sleeping with another woman! What if a man's wife desires more sex with the man that her own husband consented for her to have sex with? What if a woman' s husband desires more sex with the woman his own wife gave him permission to have sex with? At some point, jealousy is going to be the outcome, which could also lead to someone being afflicted or even murdered. Proverbs 6:32-34 tells us two important facts. First It says, "Whoso committeth adultery with a woman lacketh understanding: he that doeth it destroyeth his own soul" (v. 32). Based on the verse, any person with understanding or good sense knows the danger of adultery.

Although the verse seems to speak to a male audience, please do not think that the same doesn't apply to women also. Secondly, verse 33 and 34 says, "A wound and dishonor shall he get: and his reproach shall not be wiped away. For jealousy is the rage of a man: therefore he will not spare in the day of vengeance." Again, women become jealous too. Both men and women are wounded and even killed behind jealousy. According to verse 35, there is nothing you can give a jealous person to stop them from hurting you. Also having consent doesn't make it any less than adultery in the sight of God. Neither does it guarantee that divorce will not occur.

Hopefully, you can also see that the unrighteous give marriage a bad reputation. Their marriage dishonors God and exalts Satan. Especially the swinger married couple. Being loving and faithful to one another has to mean nothing to those who swing. It is impossible to love someone and not be faithful to them. The whole relationship is founded on lust unto the glory of Satan. The swinger adulterers do not understand the power of sex. When two people engage in sexual intercourse the act often causes them to develop feelings for one another. You can see a husband and his wife participating in sex with another married couple and soon no longer desire sex with one another after becoming one with others. Satan got a lot of people who are caught up in adultery believing that they have finally found their soulmate, just for them to leave their spouse and be unlawfully join unto another, just to find out that the grass ain't greener as they thought on the other side of the fence. Perhaps it is true to say that sex doesn't have the power to keep two people together or faithful to one another. but many are deceived to believe that sex with someone that they shouldn't be having sex with is love and is an indication that the person they're married to is not the right one. However, the fact that many are guilty of having sex with multiple people as a single person and as a married person, is proof that sex is not the key to two people getting married and remaining married until death do them apart. Therefore, the word, "soulmate" is not according to the truth. It is just another lie Satan has led so many unrighteous individuals to believe. God doesn't create us soulmates. A man is obligated to find his own wife (Proverbs 18:22). Then, if a person's spouse dies, they can be joined to another spouse, which wouldn't be possible if we have a soulmate. We were all born with freewill, the right to choose. Without it there would be no accountability.

Many rich and famous couples consent to sex with other people, and giving consent means that they do it at their own freewill. Many of them are also in and out of one marriage after the other and this is solely because of their swinging lifestyle. God is certainly dishonored by most celebrity marriages but without a relationship with God, infidelity or divorce is not surprising. It is so important that we learn from the word of God and follow the example of those who walk in obedience to Christ in their marriage. Indeed, the word of God tells us that adulterers shall not inherit the kingdom of God (1 Corinthians 6:10; Hebrews 13:4; Revelation 21:8). When people are sexually immoral, their imagination is vain, and they are foolish in their thinking. Any person who uses the excuse, "Sex with other people will keep the fire burning in our marriage" is only looking for an excuse to be unfaithful. Such a person never had any intentions of being faithful in the first place. God is extremely angry with the unrighteous and they will not go unpunished. God winks at those who are ignorant of the truth, who have not heard the gospel truth. However, those who have heard the truth, but refuse to accept that they might be saved, many of them have been sent a strong delusion (Romans 1:28; Thessalonians 2:10-12), Perhaps this explains why some continue to believe the lie that there is nothing wrong with what they're doing unto the damning of their soul. Some things are just obvious to us, and we need no one to tell us. If two people have a swinging marriage, they might be married on paper, but their marriage is nothing more than a waste of time. Chapter 16 will discuss the specifics of sex that can be enjoyed by a man and his wife.

CHAPTER 17
The Marriage Bedroom Is Undefiled

When you hear the words, "the marriage bedroom is undefiled, it simply means that sex is only approved in marriage. The bedroom is a private place, and the only people present when a man is having sex with his wife, is the man, his wife, and God. It is important for us to see God as He is. God is a Spirit and being a Spirit, God has no desire for sex.

Now, the question is, "now that I'm married, can I do sexually what I was doing prior to marriage or maybe I should simply say it this way, "what can I not do?" Some will begin at this point to insert their opinions based on their likes and dislikes about sex or search the word of God, looking for "a needle in a haystack." Well, I believe in the word of God and want to please God my Savior, by obeying what proceeded out His mouth. Stubbornly, I choose to let God be true in my life and every man a liar. Instead of getting my understanding from ungodly counselors (those whom the world seeks their advice from), I will live strictly by what is written concerning sex and marriage (Psalms 1:1-2; Matthew 4:4). What you will not find in the word of God is information on how two people can or cannot have sex in marriage. The only information we're giving is when it's not OK to have sex and who it is not OK to have sex with. As far as God is concerned, sex must be enjoyed strictly in marriage only (1 Corinthians 7:1-3). Sex with anyone other than your spouse is the overall definition of what is sexually immoral (Hebrew 13:4).

Let's be mature about sex and not put words in God's mouth or say with our own mouth what God did not say. I'm not God and I'm not going to tell you, "Oh you can't do this or that, but you can do this and that!" Besides, you're not even supposed to know what a married couple does in their bedroom and I'm certain we don't all do the things the same way to achieve sexual pleasure. However, God wouldn't dare restrict sex to marriage and not give us the how and how not to have sex if it was a major concern of His. Many people who profess to be obedient children of God are quick to say things like, "you can only have sex in the missionary position," or "oral sex is a sin," and my question to them is, "where does it state that clearly in the word of God?" False teachers intentionally add and take away from or shall I say, pervert the word of God to gain their own following and to take advantage of people, and you'll find that many of them are sexually immoral and do not practice what they teach (Acts 20:29-30; Galatians 1:6-9; Timothy 4:2). Regardless, if a person cannot back up what they say by what is written, don't listen to anything they say. The Lord our God is not the author of confusion. The standard for sex is clearly stated in the word of God.

I'm not in your bedroom at night, or peeping in your window. I don't know what you and your spouse are doing in bed at night. I'm not supposed to know nor is anyone else supposed to know. The only person that matters and He knows, is God. He's not grossed out about sex although He has no desire for it. He made it and He did it for man to enjoy with his wife (1 Corinthians 7:1-2). Surely a man that loves his wife is not going to physically, or sexually abuse his her. That would be mistreatment. Instead, he is going to do what the word of God tells us to do. He will love her as if she is his own body (Ephesians 5:28). Therefore, we nourish and cherish our wives. We love unconditionally as Christ loved the church, and gave His life for it. Furthermore, sex in marriage is a mutual thing. Neither of them can force the other to do anything that they don't feel comfortable doing. Ultimately, the children of God are led by the Spirit of God (Romans 8:14). God has a way of getting our attention and He'll do just that if we are doing something that we shouldn't be doing sexually. So far, all these years, God has not convicted me concerning anything that me and my wife regularly do for sexual pleasure. Therefore, I have no intention of stopping. Also, keep in mind that a sexual sin is a sin against the participant's own body. If what you do with your spouse causes you to reap a rash, bumps, blisters, burning, or any of the other things that are associated with sexually transmitted infections, maybe you better stop doing what you're doing. However, if sexual disease doesn't already exist, it's not going to appear out of nowhere. Regardless, if it is sin, our body will suffer in one way or another.

We must also take into consideration that a person missing a limb, arm, or leg and so on, cannot do sex the way a person with limbs can do it. Therefore, what is known as the missionary position is not going to work for everybody, but it will be necessary for some to achieve sexual pleasure in other ways. This would also mean that sex can be enjoyed in many positions. Regardless, not a single person can prove by the word of God the missionary position or any other sexual position, because it is not written.

Since such a position or any position isn't written in the word of God, how do we know about any of them? Who gave the missionary position its name? I hope from this, you conclude that sex has nothing to do with a particular position, but about the wife satisfying her husband and the husband satisfying his wife. Furthermore, what about a woman's breasts! Surely, a woman's breasts are not for breast-feeding only. Are they not also a husband's delight (Proverbs 5:19). Tell me, how does a husband delight in his wife's breasts? Is it not with his hands and with his lips, or is it sin for a husband to touch them or to put his lips on them, too! It is a known fact that women are sexually aroused at the caressing of their breasts. What about kissing, hugging, and touching one another, fondling one another, and the list goes on; is such a sin, too! Absolutely not! Foreplay is without a doubt a part of sex and those who do it, have absolutely nothing to feel guilty about unless, of course, someone can prove it to be sin by what is written.

The truth is not every word that proceeds out of man's mouth, but every word that proceeded out of God's mouth (Psalms 119:105; Matthew 4:4). It is His word that we live by. So, "Let God be true and every man a liar." A person who has a disability still has an obligation to sexually satisfy their spouse. Sex is not something that can be permanently put on whole in a marriage. In fact, we are reminded of how important sex in marriage is (1 Corinthians 7:5). So, to say that a person can't use their hand or their mouth to satisfy their spouse, would mean that those who are able to climb on top or those who are somewhat can't receive or help their spouse receive sexual satisfaction. However, those who burn with passion for sex have the gift of marriage.

There are many ways that a man and/or woman can reach the climax, the point of ejaculation, and/or orgasm. So, unless someone can give specific passages in the word of God that states that you cannot do this or that during sex in the marriage bedroom, God obviously has no problem with it. If two people stay in their own marriage bedroom and not be curious about what others do in theirs, no one can be offended by what some do because they'll have no knowledge of it. Remember, we are to be perfect (mature) as God is perfect. So, enjoy sex and marriage. Chapter 17 will deal with why marriage is not for everyone and what is the evidence.

CHAPTER 18
Marriage: Necessary for Some but not for Others

Beware of false teachers, those who have been seduced by lying spirits and doctrines of demons. There are many who teach people to do things that they do not do themselves (1 Timothy 4:1-2). If it is the will of God and we teach it as such, we are obligated to practice it also. In fact, the children of God are both, hearers, and doers of the word of God (Matthew 7:21; Luke 8:21; James 1:22). What we don't ever want to do is cause others to stumble by what we teach, and whatever we teach we must be able to back it up by what is written in the word of God, or the person teaching proves to be a liar. Since there are so many who teach falsely for their own selfish reasons, we must try every spirit to see if they are of God (Matthew 24:11; Acts 20:29-30; Galatians 1:6-9; 1 Timothy 4:1-2; 1 John 4:1). Ultimately, those who represent God are not going to intentionally add to or take away from what the Lord spoke and what His appointed witnesses confirmed (Acts 10:39-42; Hebrews 2:3). We are students of the word of God and rightly dividing the word of truth is our top priority (2 Timothy 2:15). Also, the children of God have received from God the Spirit of truth also known as the spirit of Christ and the Holy Spirit (John 14:17; 1 Corinthians 6:19; Ephesians 1:13-14). He is not optional and every person that doesn't have Him, doesn't belong to the Lord (Romans 8:9). He teaches us all things and brings all things back unto our remembrance what is written in the word of God (Matthew 4:4; John 14:26). Now that we are clear that we can't believe every word spoken from the mouth of men! The question is, is marriage necessary for everybody? If not, what is the evidence that a person should marry or doesn't need to marry? Any person who teaches people that they are forbidden to marry are false teachers (1 Timothy 4:1-3; 1 Corinthians 7:7). We must remember that God established marriage as a necessary institution in the very beginning (Genesis 2:24). He determined that man should not be alone and created man, a wife to serve as his helper (Genesis 2:18). If there were no male and female relationships from the very beginning, we wouldn't have a world filled with people, today. Sexual intercourse is the way it's accomplished. However, God is against people having sex outside of marriage. So, to avoid fornication, it is the will of God that two people get married (1 Corinthians 7:1-2). Marriage is good and honorable in the sight of God (Hebrews 13:4). However, marriage is not desired by everybody, but how do we know who it's for? It's simple! If a person burns with passion for the opposite sex, marriage is for them. On the other hand, if a person does not burn with passion it is not for them. When the word of God is rightly divided, it reveals to us that marriage is a gift for some and not for others. Now, before someone assumes that God is a respecter of persons, let me clarify. Jesus said, "For there are some eunuchs, which were so born from their mother's womb: and there are some eunuchs, which were made eunuchs of men: and there be eunuchs, which have made themselves eunuchs for the kingdom of heaven's sake" (Matthew 19:12). Based on the verse, there are three ways that a man or person will not have a desire for sex. There is spiritual castration, so to speak. These are individuals born without the desire for sex. Then, there are men who have been physically castrated by other men. Lastly, Some men castrated themselves so that they can be more devoted unto God. What is most important to understand is, if a man is ever physically castrated, he'll not be able to have sex.

Paul, an apostle of Jesus Christ, was also a single man. He obviously had no desire for a woman whether he was born without or castrated at some point in his life. He reveals this to us in his letter to the Corinthians. In 1 Corinthians , chapter 7, Paul writes, "For I would that all men were even as I myself. But every man hath his proper gift of God, one after this manner, and another after that" (v. 7). The verse alone is telling us that marriage is not for everybody. In the very next verse, Paul tells that for the sake of serving God, remaining single gives us more time to devote to God, if the person can contain themselves (v.8).

We also learn that everybody does have the power to do it. Some will burn with the passion for sex. However, there are some who are unmarried who can and will remain unmarried. For example, some widows, women up in age lose the desire for sex, and because they do, they don't ever marry again. Regardless, the person who has a desire to have sex is only to enjoy it in a marriage. This is not what false teachers teach. Any doctrine that teaches that a person MUST NOT GET MARRIED is not according to the truth. It is a doctrine of demons, as Paul calls it (1 Timothy 4:1-3). False teachers have no intention of obeying what they teach others not to do. Their objective is to intentionally cause people to stumble OUT OF THE FAITH.

Many of the people who take heed to the false teachers, end up in fornication, because they burn with the passion sex while at the same convince that it is sin for them to marry. As I have already mentioned, many religious leaders, who teach a doctrine that is not according to the truth, are sexually immoral people. They practice masturbation, engage in sex with underage children, and practice homosexuality. Just imagine how many women become nuns and how many men become priests, who have the gift of marriage, but because of their religious position they are forbidden to marry. A person's ability to abstain from sex is not by their own might or power, but it's by the power of the Holy Spirit. Those who engage in forbidden sexuality can never blame God for why they engage in masturbation, homosexuality, and pedophilia. Forbidding to marry is by choice and not forced upon anyone. The truth is not hidden from any of us. In fact, false teachers specialize in convincing people that the truth they've already heard is a lie and what they teach is the truth. Furthermore, hypocrites appear as sheep when in public by their false humility and their holy and modest apparel. However, behind closed doors, they do what they teach others they ought not do. It's that they are the least concerned about what God thinks and more concerned about what people think. Perhaps this is because they're not trying to win souls with what they teach. They know that what they teach is false. In exchange for doing the lust of their father, the devil, they are rewarded monetary gain. So, if you are thinking that marriage is sin for some, hopefully you're now convinced that it is the will of God that those who desire sex get married. Chapter 18 will reveal whether you are guilty of encouraging others to be sexually immoral.

CHAPTER 19
It Is Our Duty to Expose and Warn People About Sexual Sin

As believers in the Lord Jesus Christ, we have an obligation to tell people the truth and to raise our children up in the way of the Lord. This, we must do without compromise, just as the Lord our God does not compromise. For example, Jesus our Lord said these words, "except a person repents they shall perish" (Luke 13:1-5, KJV). Such a statement doesn't give us any room for sin. Repentance doesn't imply that we should stop committing certain things that God hates, but rather, that we must stop practicing sin altogether. Therefore, there is no safe way to sin because the Lord doesn't offer us a safe way to do it. He doesn't say to us, "Well, I don't want you to sin, but if you sin, be safe.

Yes, our God is just to forgive if we commit a sinful act, but we must never give others the impression by what we say that it is OK to sin (Romans 6:1-2; Galatians 5:13-16; 1 John 2:1). Sin is not something that is to be done responsibly. That is because it is not something that can be done responsibly. Everytime a person commits sin they are taken a risk. Absolutely nothing can come out of it. I mention all this to say that we must make sure that we're not guilty of encouraging others to sin by what we do and say. As a father, I emphasize to my children that they are not to engage in fornication and if they do, they will reap what they sow. I explained to them what it means to sin against their own body. They understand that there are diseases that can be contracted from engaging in fornication and that boys can get girls pregnant. Not once have I told them or anybody else to be careful why you're sinning. However, I've come to realize that a lot of professed believers do tell their children and others not to have sex. Then, they turn around to make what they said to them null and void, because in the next breath they say to them, "if you're going to be having sex, make sure you protect yourself." Now, if we tell people to protect themselves after telling them what is not to sin, we have pretty told them to sin responsibly. As a result, we cause them to stumble. The point is, sexual sin doesn't become something less than what God says it is simply because the female uses birth control and/or the male wears a condom. Should believers put their daughters on birth control and buy their sons condoms! Do we think they're not going to use it! Do we not think they're going to think that they are protected because of what we provided them with! Well, are they really safe and if so, where does it say so in the word of God that we say live by. The question we should ask ourselves is, "Do we want our children and others to repent of sin or not!" If we fail to tell them the truth as it is written, they will have the wrong perception of sin.

What did Jesus mean when He said, "Repent?" What did Jesus men when told the woman caught in the act of adultery, "Go away and sin no more?" The words give clarity to what it means to repent. Therefore, we must speak the truth as clear as Jesus did it. He told us that to follow Him, we must deny ourselves, take up our cross daily and follow Him (Luke 9:23). So, what does it mean to deny ourselves? Isn't the Lord telling that we have to die to the desires of the flesh? Indeed, He is. Therefore, we must be straightforward with people. As believers, we know that there are consequences for sexual disobedience. We also know that the only way to avoid them is by not having sex.

We want people to be afraid to do it, not thinking that there are ways around the consequences. Besides, the consequences for people's disobedience are necessary to get their attention. They make people think twice before participating in sexual sin again. No, consequences will not stop everybody but it will deter some unto the glory of God. Besides, what would be the purpose of stopping if it was possible to reap corruption!. If we don't want people to be destroyed behind sexual pleasure, we must tell them what God says about it. If they refuse to hear us, the suffering is deserving. It will prove to them that we told them not to do it because we love them.

It all boils down to, who do we love more, people or God. However, every believer is aware of what the word of God teaches, and therefore, we must love God above all else and avoid watering down the truth (Matthew 10:37-38). The most important commandment is, "Love God our Lord with all of our heart, soul, and mind," but how can we do this if we compromise our faith for the people we love (Matthew 22:37). We want to be counted worthy to inherit the kingdom of God. Does it make you happy when you hear about the rise in sexually transmitted disease! How would you feel if your son came home when an infection after using the condom that you encouraged him to use to protect himself! What about your daughter who was concerned about getting pregnant, but didn't stop to think that birth control doesn't protect against sexual infections. There are countless young people parenting children and dealing with sexual infections because society has given them the impression that having sex is normal for young people. "Be not conformed to this world" is the will of God, not follow the crowd through the wide gate and down the broad road that leads to destruction (Matthew 7:13). Instead, we must direct people through the straight gate and the narrow that leads to eternal life. Well, what's wrong with having, some young people might say. What's wrong is babies are born out of wedlock. Then there is HIV/AIDS, herpes, genital warts, cervical cancer, gonorrhea, chlamydia, and who knows what else. So is experiencing sex or enjoying sexual pleasure really worth the risk! I don't know about you, but I do not want anyone's blood on my hands. Neither do I want my children to suffer and be able to say that I didn't tell them not to have sex or that these things would happen. We must not encourage dating or encourage them to get them a girlfriend or boyfriend. What are they needed for when the only person you're obligated to be faithful to and provide sexual pleasure is the person you marry. Can we love the Lord and be OK with our son or daughter hugging, kissing, and having sex with someone? Not if we believe in the word of God. It says, "It is good for a man not to touch a woman. To avoid fornication get married (1 Corinthians 7:1-2). If we know what touching and kissing can lead to, we will not encourage any person who is not married to do it, child or adult. In these last days, people do not have a desire to sound doctrine just as it is written (2 Timothy 4:3). Men and women are living together like husband and wife and they're never told that it's wrong for them to be living together, not married. Many women and girls are getting pregnant as a result of fornication, and their family and friends say to them, "Congratulations" like it is a good thing to have children out of wedlock. So you see, it is our duty as the people of God to expose sin just as Jesus did to the Samaritan woman at the well. He called her a fornicator and an adulterer (John 4:16-18). Paul also made it clear who would not inherit the kingdom of God (1 Corinthians 6:9; Galatians 5:19). In both passages, fornication and adultery is mentioned. We are guilty of encouraging people when we neglect to tell them and when we give them a watered down version because we don't want to offend anyone. That's called fear and the word says that cowards (the fearful) shall not inherit the kingdom of God (Revelation 21:8). In the book of Matthew, Jesus puts it a different way. He said, "Fear not man who can only destroy the body. Rather fear God, who can destroy the body and the soul in Hell" (Matthew 10:28). If we keep our mouth shut and say nothing about the things that God hates, we obviously do not believe what the verse says. God cannot lie and He does not change.

The truth is, everyone is not going to turn from sin, but we can't be afraid to tell people the truth concerning sin. We can't support sin. We encourage sin. We can continue in sin. We are the mouthpieces of God. We are His representatives, His children, and His servants unto the glory of our Father. We please God, not people. The world will hate us, even members of our own household. Let us not assume that children are too young to learn about the will of God. We have an obligation to train them up (Proverb 22:6). Jesus loves the children and doesn't want us to keep them from coming to Him (Matthew 19:14). Lastly, if you have lived a sexually immoral lifestyle, you also have experienced consequences for sexual sin. Therefore, you know the danger of engaging in sexual sin, and therefore, God would have us to encourage people not to do, both the youth and the adults, that by our preaching some will choose to be dead to sin and alive to God.

CHAPTER 20
Forgiveness and Healing Go Hand and Hand

Everyone will have a sinful experience in this sinful world. After we are given the time to engage in, God hopes that we will become so frustrated in life that we long to have the void inside of us, permanently satisfied. No matter how long we indulge in sinful pleasure, it never satisfies us. Instead, we pursue the pleasure thereof over and over chasing that which never comes, fulfillment. However, the good feeling that we get from sinful pleasure, produces many bad results that cause us unwanted pain and sorrow. However, all that we suffer because of sin is not God's will for our life although He allows it with reason. Instead of desiring sin, God wants us to seek after Him. He longs to have fellowship with us. Therefore, He hopes that the side-effects of sin causes us to seek Him though He is not far from any of us (Acts 17:27). He loves so much that He doesn't allow the experience of sin to destroy us because He is aware that we are ignorant to what he thinks about the things we do. So just as Paul writes in the book of Acts, "And the times of this ignorance God winked at; but now commanded all men everywhere to repent" (17:30).

However, before a person can repent, they must first hear the truth that comes from God. It alone has the power to forgive sin and save us all by grace. This truth and the grace that saves us came to us by Jesus Christ (John 1:17). The truth is a message of love. We have it in written form and those who have heard the truth unto repentance continue to speak it so that others may hear it and be set free from the bondage sin and be saved. Perhaps, some will say at this point, "Saved from what?" Well, saved from God's wrath that shall be poured out upon all who take pleasure in unrighteousness. Indeed, it is not the will of God that any should perish. Instead, it is God's will that all come to repentance (2 Peter 3:9).

As the offspring of God, we were created for Him (Colossians 1:16). We were created to be in His image and after His likeness (Genesis 1:26). Therefore, our ways are supposed to be His ways and how thoughts are supposed to be His thoughts. The children are supposed to be like their father, who loves us and gives us life. He wants us to love also, with all our heart, soul, and mind, and love one another as we love ourselves (Matthew 22:37-40). To love Him is to obey Him and to love one another is to do unto others as we would have others to do unto us (Matthew 7:12). However, the first thing we must do is admit that we are guilty of living a lifestyle that God hates. Then, we must believe in Jesus Christ, who shed His blood that we might receive forgiveness of sin. This is what it means when it says, "For God so loved the world that He gave His only begotten Son that whosoever believes in Him, shall not perish but shall have everlasting life" (John 3:16).

Those who believe in Him become followers of Him. However, to follow Him, one must die to the practice of sin and take up their cross (Luke 9:23). In other words, we are saved by grace that we receive through faith in Jesus Christ. Those who receive the grace cannot continue in sin, which God hates. This is because they are dead to sin and alive to God (Romans 6::1-2). We must live a new life in Christ. a life that is spiritual and fulfills not the lust of the flesh. The old us passess away (2 Corinthians 5:17). To be a new creature in Christ, we have to give sexually immoral ways. We must be willing to enjoy sex only in the marriage bedroom. Anything that God hates is not good for us and as our Father, He wants what is best for His children. Indeed, God is not pleased when we disobey Him, but it hurts Him to see us suffer the consequences for sin. However, as our Father, God cannot tolerate disobedience. We all have an appointment with death and if we die before dying to sin and become alive unto God, the opportunity we have now to be saved by grace will no longer be available to us. Will you receive the love of the truth or will you refuse it? Will you come in the light where God is that you might enjoy fellowship with Him and some day receive the gift of eternal life. Or, will you continue in the pleasure of unrighteousness? God wants to heal you by His blood which He shed for you on the cross. Only you can choose to be free. Only you can choose to be healed of the sin in your heart. Only you can continue to receive God's gift of eternal life. It is my prayer that you choose wisely.

About the Author

My name is Bro. Lamont Wall. I am a member of the body of Christ. I was delivered from a sexually immoral lifestyle by the power of God Almighty. Being redeemed by the blood of the precious Lamb, Jesus Christ, I have an obligation to live according to the truth of the word of God unto the glory of God. As a servant of the Lord, I am a vessel used by Him to plant and water the word of God in the hearing of those who are humble enough to hear unto knowledge, wisdom, and understanding that they too, might be redeemed and added to the Lord's church, which is His body. I'm also a working man, a husband and father, living a simple lifestyle, in a small city in North Carolina where I was also born and raised. Fishing, spending time with my wife and children, writing, and teaching the word of God is the summary of my life and I am content with having what I need from day to day.